Joe,

I value your leadership,
direction, and support.
Thanks for your words of
encouragement, for your important
and significant role on our
USA church-planting team. It
is a joy and privilege to be your
friend and compatriot in the
Great Commission!

Jay 3/7/90.

BOARDROOM CONFIDENCE

BOARDROOM CONFIDENCE
© 1988 by Bobb Biehl and Ted W. Engstrom
Published by Questar Publishers, Inc.

Second Printing, 1989

Printed in the United States of America

ISBN 0-945564-06-6

Cover design by Bruce DeRoos

Library of Congress Cataloging-in-Publication Data

Engstrom, Theodore Wilhelm
Biehl, Bobb
Boardroom confidence.

1. Church management. 2. Management.
I. Biehl, Bobb. II. Title.
BV652.E618 1988   254   88-18264
ISBN 0-945564-06-6

Increasing Your

BOARDROOM
CONFIDENCE

Bobb Biehl & Ted W. Engstrom

QUESTAR PUBLISHERS, INC.

SISTERS, OREGON

CONTENTS

Appendix:

INTRODUCTION

**_ESSENCE:_ _Let our combined experience_
help you succeed!**

AS YOU CONSIDER your responsibilities as a board member...
have you ever wished you could sit down and chat with
someone who had a wealth of experience on many boards—a
mentor who could answer your many questions, show you
the ropes, show you how to be more confident and effective
in your position on the board?

NOW YOU HAVE SOMEONE TO HELP YOU!

We have a combined experience of fifty years serving
more than eighty boards. We've spent thousands of hours
making decisions, solving problems, choosing senior executives, and all the things that go with being on a board. Har-
nessing that experience to further your success as a
confident board member, board chairman, or senior executive will bring us great pleasure.

When we say *you,* we mean *you!* If you're a new board
member, we mean you. If you've been on a board for thirty
years and just want to be more effective, we mean you. If
you're a board chairman and want to be more efficient at
running board meetings and more adept in working with
people, we mean you. If you're a senior executive (a CEO,

senior pastor, executive director) and you want to learn how to work more closely and productively with your board—and to help your staff do the same—we mean you. Or if you simply hope to be a board member some day, we mean you.

For simplicity in this book we'll often use as a model the local church board. We're going to assume you're a member of a church board and want to be a better member. This seems a reasonable assumption since you are probably a member of a church and either serve on the church board or have an interest in its effectiveness.

You will quickly see, however, that the principles for gaining boardroom confidence are surprisingly alike regardless of the board you're on—for a church or Christian organization, a for-profit corporation, or a community-based nonprofit service agency.

Whether your board involvement is in serving a small church or a Fortune 500 company, our hope is that by reading this book you'll have more "boardroom confidence" for the rest of your life.

Section A
UNDERSTANDING THE
ENTIRE BOARD PROCESS

ESSENCE: *The BOARDROOM CONFIDENCE Progress Chart shows you where to begin—and what to do next.*

FUNDAMENTAL TO YOUR understanding of how all the pieces fit together in boardroom effectiveness is what we call the "Board Process." On the next page you'll find a chart showing an overview of this process—beginning with Board Basics and continuing through Advanced Training for the Senior Executive. Truly grasping the Board Process is so critical to board

The BOARD PROCESS Chart
(Numbers correspond to chapter numbers in *Boardroom Confidence*)

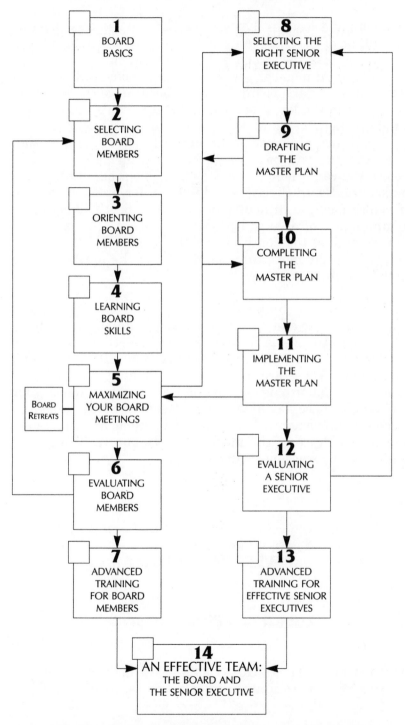

As a record of your progress, check off (✔) the box for each chapter as you read it.

members and leaders that we've chosen to use this chart as the outline of the book. As you'll see, the first chapter is Step 1 in the process, the second is Step 2, and so on.

As a board member you want to keep constantly in mind this overview of the board...so you'll never have the feeling of being lost in the forest of board business details. Each piece will have more meaning when its overall context is clear.

You'll also notice that the Board Process is sequential. For example, you have to select board members (Step 2) before you can orient them (Step 3). This sequential nature makes the Board Process a helpful tool for problem solving. If you're facing a difficulty in Step 5 or 6, it's likely to be symptomatic of a causal problem in Steps 4, 3, or 2. By understanding the continuity of the overall Board Process, you will be far more capable of solving the most common problems within any board.

You've heard the maxim: "Never re-invent the wheel." We would like to add, "...but never stop refining the tire!" In board operations—as in any area of life—there are a few fundamental pieces in the process that you will use over and over again. These are the steps that should be refined year after year. You are never wasting time as you enhance your abilities in these key areas, no matter how many times you pursue improvement. The better you become at each step in the Board Process, the more effective and fulfilling your entire board experience will be.

Section B
INVEST IN YOURSELF

ESSENCE: *Be a lifelong student.*

YOU MAY NOT FEEL CONFIDENT as a board member today, but as you read through this book and continue reading, learning, and growing, in a few years you can be making an exceptional contribution. See yourself as a lifelong student, continually improving your effectiveness as a board member. Invest time, energy and money as needed in the pursuit of excellence. As you grow stronger, the board grows stronger, and the entire organization grows stronger.

Some members see their board responsibilities as something like a prison term—they're working out their sentence. Don't let yourself be caught in that trap. Begin taking initiative to grow as a board member to the point that you can provide leadership even in the most unlikely of situations.

Investing in your development as a board member increases your ability to lead anywhere at any time. Make learning to lead a lifelong personal goal.

Section C
ADAPT...DON'T ADOPT

Essence: Adopting "as is" the information in this book is not wise. ADAPTING the information to fit your own situation IS wise.

IN THIS BOOK we have included a number of examples and illustrations, but they'll not all be equally helpful to you. Not every chapter will meet your present need as a board member. Pick and choose what will help you now, and see BOARDROOM CONFIDENCE as a reference book for the future. What may not seem important now may become very important later. Use what you need when you need it.

Take what we have developed and adapt it to your board. It is far easier to develop your own checklist or profile or position description if you have a draft from which to begin. View this book as a "first draft" version of your own "personal" edition.

You'll have experiences unique to your board. Each time you go through something new, get in the habit of "marking your trail" by writing down the things you learn. Each time you select a new board member, for example, use our board selection process as a model—but improve it by recording your own observations, and keep improving it so it becomes far better than what we have suggested. KEEP MARKING YOUR TRAIL!

SUMMARY

To help you increase your boardroom confidence:

1. View us as being here to help *you* succeed.

2. Keep clearly in mind the Board Process (you'll see the diagram of it reprinted at the beginning of each chapter in this book).

3. Invest in yourself as a lifelong student.

4. Adapt—don't just adopt—the information in this book.

Now it's time to start learning the Board Process.

The BOARD PROCESS Chart
FOR BOARDROOM CONFIDENCE

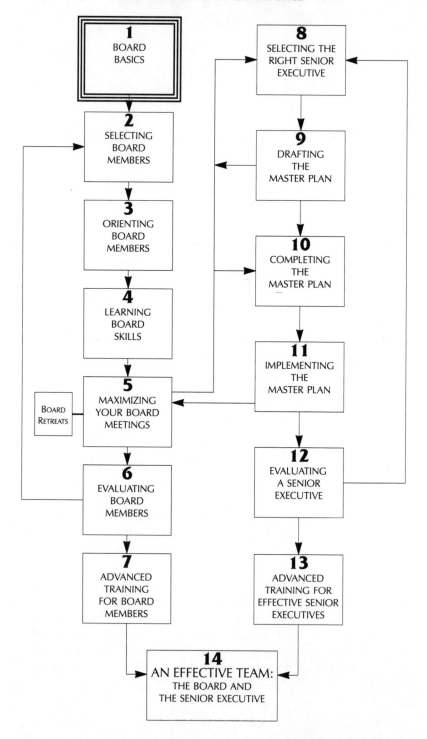

AGREEING ON BOARD BASICS

ESSENCE: Brand the board basics into your brain...and your heart.

MASTER THE BOARD BASICS ONCE, and they'll guide you for many decades of boardroom service.

Section A
AGREEING ON BASIC TERMS

ESSENCE: All miscommunication is the result of differing assumptions.

MANY PEOPLE think of a typical board as a Super Bowl team sharing a special vocabulary, common plans, and years of working together. In fact, a board is more often like an All-Star team that brings together the best and the brightest from a variety of backgrounds. A board often will include members from business, industry, military, education, and other professions all represented in one room. Frequently, few or none of these team members will have extensive experience playing together. Therefore, few of them use the same words to mean the same thing. That's a situation ripe for trouble, because, as Dr. Jerry Ballard, president of the World Relief Commission, points out: "All miscommunication is the result of differing assumptions."

For the sake of shared assumptions—and thus, good communication—discuss with other board members the meaning of terms commonly used by your board. Agree as a board on ten to twenty basic words for which you have a common, everyday understanding of their appropriate use. This will help you avoid misunderstandings, frustration, and tension during your entire board tenure.

Here is a selection of terms heard frequently in the boardroom, with simple definitions:

1. AD HOC COMMITTEE—a small group of people (three to five) who are asked to take on a small, short-term assignment—for example, drafting a Position Focus Sheet for a new position within the organization.

2. AUTHORITY—the ability to make a final decision without asking anyone else.

> Within your organization there should be clear limits of authority for the staff and volunteers. Everyone needs to know what he or she can decide without asking someone else. Every staff member and volunteer needs some degree of authority to carry out assigned responsibility.
>
> These limits of authority need to be progressive. For example, when a person has been in a new position for a month, he may have an authority spending limit (for petty cash, charging, contractual commitments, check writing) of $50. When he's been there a year, the limit could be $500, and after ten years $1,000 or $10,000. Whatever the authority limit is, it should be clearly stated in his Position Focus Sheet (or job description).
>
> You've heard the phrase "responsibility without au-

thority" in reference to someone who's been given a task to do, but no authority to make necessary decisions to carry it out. Be sure that with any assignment you make you also give the appropriate corresponding authority. If you ask an assistant to buy a case of file folders, he needs to be able to spend the money for them.

3. ETHICS—principles of acceptable, standard practice for behavior and actions.

As a board member, understand clearly the distinctions between what is ethical, what is moral, and what is legal. *Ethics* are relative to the immediate environment— to local and cultural standards of business, for example. *Morals,* on the other hand, are based on an absolute standard—the Bible. *Legality* is based on coded law.

If something is *illegal*...it violates the law.
If it's *immoral*...it violates a Biblical standard.
If it's *unethical*...it does not conform to standard, acceptable practice.

4. MASTER PLAN—a written statement of assumptions about our direction, organization, and resources.

5. POLICY—what we always do or what we never do.

Setting policy allows a board to help staff members make some decisions automatically within certain guidelines. Financial policy, for example, is what we always do or what we never do when it comes to money. If a board's financial policy states, "We never allow our bills to be due beyond thirty days," the staff member with a bill thirty-one days old knows he should not wait to pay it...the decision to pay is automatic.

6. STANDING COMMITTEE (or SUB-COMMITTEE) —an ongoing group of people responsible for a specific area of the organization—the budget, for example.

7. STEERING COMMITTEE (or ORGANIZING COMMITTEE)—a small group of people who start something before a legal board has been formed to oversee it.

8. TASK FORCE—a short-term group responsible for some major project with a definite goal and ending point. An example: the annual picnic task force.

You may want to add your own definitions to the eight terms above. You will also want to discuss and define perhaps ten to twenty additional words that are frequently used in your own organizational setting.

Be sure to keep the definitions practical. Avoid hard-to-follow philosophical explanations.

Many boards do not understand the value of defining a few basic terms clearly. You may want to take it upon yourself to listen for those words which tend to cause miscommunication. Write out your own definitions for them, hand them out at a meeting...and see what results.

Section B
AGREEING ON BOARD MEMBER ROLES
AND RESPONSIBILITIES

ESSENCE: Do what is expected
of you...and you gain credibility.
Don't do what is expected of you...
and you lose credibility.

EVERY BOARD or group you choose to work with will have different expectations about the role you're to play and the responsibilities you're to carry out ...and that's all right. What isn't all right is failing to define exactly what is expected of each member —which is wasting the best opportunity to increase everyone's level of comfort and confidence.

Below we've spelled out ten of the most frequent roles and responsibilities we've seen boards include in their thinking. Use these as a discussion guideline (rather than simply adopting them with little thought) to help you determine what your group sees as its roles and responsibilities.

You also may want to discuss at length the order of priority these roles and responsibilities will have with your board (to avoid implying our own personal priorities, our list here is in alphabetical order, according to the key words in each item).

1. APPRECIATING, RECOGNIZING, and ENCOURAGING everyone who makes a contribution in the group.

One of the most "contagious" roles of the board is appreciating, encouraging and recognizing the senior executive, the executive staff (paid or volunteer), and others who make a positive contribution.

Typically, the senior executive looks to the board for appreciation and encouragement, the staff looks to the senior executive, and the constituents look to the staff. But we've found that "you can't give what you don't have." If a senior executive or staff member is not encouraged, it is very difficult for him to give others the appreciation they look for from him.

If he *is* appreciated, encouraged, and recognized, he finds it much easier to do so for those around him, who in turn find it easier to do so throughout the rest of the organization.

The board member is one of the leaders in any organization who must *concentrate* on making everyone feel appreciated, encouraged and recognized for their contributions. As you play this role effectively, the morale of the organization will remain consistently higher. (See Chapter Four, Section A for more about this.)

2. DECISION MAKING.

In three main areas the board will need to make decisions:

a) *directional* (the purpose of your organization—its goals and plans)
b) *organizational* (who joins the staff and who does not, how the staff is structured, etc.)
c) *financial*

Keeping these three areas distinct in your own mind will help you focus on board priorities. (See Chapter Four, Section F.)

3. Reviewing, refining, approving, and tracking the MASTER PLAN.

Earlier we defined the Master Plan as "a written statement of assumptions about our direction, organization, and resources." Trying to develop a thriving organization without a Master Plan is like running a race without a finish line. You have no points of reference, no direction, no track to run on, no way of marking your progress. (The Master Plan process is discussed thoroughly in Chapters Nine through Eleven.)

4. NETWORKING—bringing appropriate resources to bear on the need at hand.

We have found that *people* are the greatest resource of any organization. Whenever the board faces a problem, the right *people* are typically the solution. Therefore, one of the most valuable assets you bring to the board is the network of people you know. You have contacts—among community leaders and sources of outside funding, for example—that no one else in your group may have.

There are times, of course, when the appropriate resource for meeting a present need is your own personal expertise and background.

5. Keeping an OVERVIEW of the entire organization.

It is critical—fundamental—for each board member to

keep an overview of the entire organization and not just his or her favorite part. Your focus as a board is on what's best for the entire organization—especially since most staff members tend to get so busy pruning and nurturing their own tree that they lose track of the forest. (See Chapter Four, Section M.)

1

Here are three ways you can keep a "full-forest" view:

a. Keep track of the Master Plan, especially the directional statement, the organizational chart, and the financial trend charts.

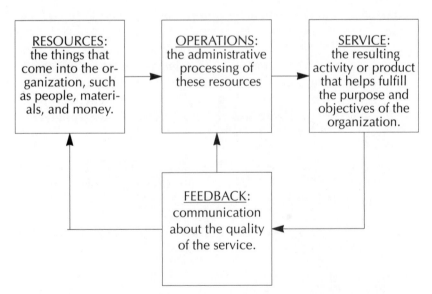

This cycle of interrelated processes is evident on many levels in an organization. In a church, for example, contributions (a resource) are received, the money is deposited, receipted and allocated (operations), and then spent on a budgeted activity (service is carried out). Later reports (feedback) to the board and the church's administrative team detail the full process.

b. Maintain a balance in size and scope among the different parts that together make up the ongoing "life" of your organization.

Every organization can ultimately be analyzed in four basic elements or categories or steps of action. These four are resources, operations, service, and feedback, as defined in the diagram on page 25.

Ultimately the entire organization will be affected by any imbalance in these areas.

c. Keep an "outside-in" perspective on your organization. Try to see your organization with an outsider's objectivity, rather than an insider's subjectivity.

6. PROBLEM SOLVING.

Three primary areas of problem solving are likely to face you as a board member.

a. You may be asked to help solve problems the senior executive and staff do not feel capable of solving alone. These are often problems that call for new policies, or that require more business experience than the staff has.

b. You may be asked to help solve a community relations problem that the senior executive feels uncomfortable handling.

c. You may be asked to help solve a problem within the board itself.

(See Chapter Four, Section Q.)

7. RECORD KEEPING.

It is the board's responsibility to make sure records in these four areas are maintained and updated regularly:

a. constitution and bylaws
b. policy and procedure manual
c. board minutes
d. financial records

(See Chapter Four, Section J.)

8. The SENIOR EXECUTIVE—hiring, evaluating, and releasing.

Your organization's senior executive is a directional leader who—if it's the wrong person at this time for the job —can cost the board and the organization dearly. (You'll find comprehensive information on hiring senior executives in Chapter Eight, and on evaluating and releasing an executive in Chapter Twelve.)

9. Providing SPIRITUAL LEADERSHIP.

Board members for churches are morally obligated to meet the biblical qualifications for eldership, and to provide the spiritual leadership expected of elders, according to scriptural teaching. But spiritual qualifications and leadership expectations are likely to mean something else to boards serving organizations other than churches. In either of these situations, however, you and the other board members will profit greatly by discussing at length what it means to provide spiritual leadership within the context of your organization.

10. Maintaining a STANDARD OF EXCELLENCE.

One simple way to impress on the board the need to maintain a standard of excellence in the organization is to bring to a board meeting toy models of a Volkswagen Beetle, Chevrolet, Buick, Cadillac, Mercedes, and Rolls-Royce. Ask the other board members which class of automobile they feel best represents what you together want your organization to be. Are you a "VW Bug" organization or are you a Rolls-Royce organization? This is not a very technical way of getting at this issue, but it can be a practical and enduring way.

How many times have you walked into an office, met the organization's staff or leaders, and noticed the excellence with which business is conducted there? On the other hand,

---

Ten Key Roles and Responsibilities for Board Members

1. APPRECIATING, RECOGNIZING, and ENCOURAGING everyone who makes a contribution in the group.

2. DECISION MAKING.

3. Reviewing, refining, approving, and tracking the MASTER PLAN.

4   NETWORKING—bringing appropriate resources to bear on the need at hand.

5. Keeping an OVERVIEW of the entire organization.

6. PROBLEM SOLVING.

7. RECORD KEEPING.

8. The SENIOR EXECUTIVE—hiring, evaluating, and releasing.

9. Providing SPIRITUAL LEADERSHIP.

10. Maintaining a STANDARD OF EXCELLENCE.

How would you rank these roles and responsibilities in their importance for your board?

---

how often have you walked in and sensed the lack of excellence?

Maintaining your organization's standard of excellence is primarily a responsibility of the staff, but as a board member you can be supportive of every initiative they take in upgrading standards for contact with the public, overall appearance, communication style, and much more. For example, it's difficult for a person from a "first-class" home (clean, neat, well maintained) to attend regularly a "third-class" church (poorly cleaned, cluttered, needing new paint, and so on).

(See Chapter Four, Section I.)

NO MATTER HOW your board defines your responsibilities, being on a board can be a great experience—exciting, challenging, and fulfilling. While enjoying a position of honor, you can bring direction and efficiency to your organization. You can help it make the most of its resources...to uncover breakthrough ideas...and to find a bright future.

Section C
AGREEING ON BOARD BEDROCK

ESSENCE: Base your decisions on biblical bedrock—on eternal wisdom and truth— and not on passing fads or contemporary culture.

YOUR BOARD'S INTERPRETATION of what the Bible says, and your assumptions about what a term or phrase in business usage means, may differ considerably from the views on the board of a church or organization across town. But it is critical that each of you NOT differ greatly from the member sitting next to you. This is not to say you have to force every member to think about every topic just like you do. Yet, it is vital to arrive at unanimous agreement on what your board's position will be on Scripture, on biblical precepts, and on the role of the board.

For example, decisions about character traits you will look for in prospective board members will typically be based on biblical passages such as 1 Timothy 3 and Titus 3. Decide in advance how to interpret and apply these criteria. In so doing you will lay a strong foundation on which to build your organization, a foundation with these twin cornerstones:

SCRIPTURE: bedrock for decision making

CHARACTER: bedrock for board membership

SUMMARY

Since "all miscommunication is a result of differing assumptions," the entire board, the senior executive, and executive staff (paid or volunteer) should make sure they have the same assumptions about:

a) the terms you're using.

b) the roles and responsibilities you share.

c) the bedrock truths you agree on.

As you reinforce your singlemindedness in these areas, there will be fewer miscommunications and more successes. You'll notice a major reduction in the frustration and tension that can otherwise clog the boardroom atmosphere. And a clearer sense of team unity is a certain by-product.

YOU'VE NOW COMPLETED Step 1 in the Board Process as outlined in the chart on page 13. For your own feeling of progress, you may want to indicate your completion of this chapter by checking [✔] the first box on the chart.

Next is Step 2—one of the most critical steps for boardroom confidence.

The **BOARD PROCESS** Chart
For Boardroom Confidence

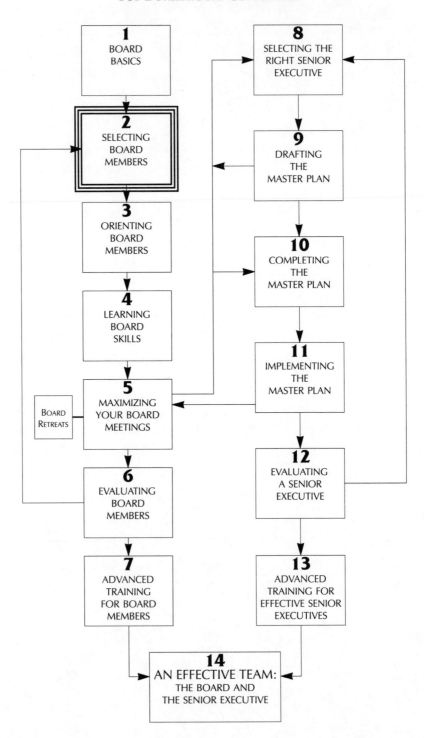

2

SELECTING BOARD MEMBERS

ESSENCE: If you have the right board members, the right things happen. If you have the wrong board members, the wrong things happen.

YOUR SECOND CRITICAL STEP in the board process—the step on which everything else ultimately depends—is getting the right board members together. As you become more effective at the membership selection process, the board will become increasingly stronger. As we discussed earlier, the stronger the board, the stronger the organization; the stronger the organization, the greater its contribution in history.

Section A
STAYING WITH THE PROCESS

ESSENCE: The best time to fire a person is when you don't hire him. Likewise, the best time to ask a board member to resign is when you don't select him for membership.

As a board and as leaders, master the skill of selecting the right people for the right positions. From noted author Dr. R. C. Sproul, president of the Ligonier Valley Study Center, we've heard the phrase, "The best time to fire a person is when you don't hire him." The same is true with board members. The selection step is the start or end of ninety percent of your future board problems.

Below you'll find an outline of the Selection Process for New Board Members. If you apply all the steps indicated in this process, you'll have the best chance of getting precisely the new member you're looking for, rather than someone

Selection Process for New Board Members

1. Board appoints nominating committee.

2. Committee reviews...

   a. the Board Member Profile (character qualities and expertise; see Section B).

   b. the Board Position Focus Sheet (a job description; see Section C, and the sample in the Appendix).

   c. the selection process outlined here.

3. Committee draws up list of possible candidates.

   Before you start asking potential candidates if they would be open to serving, be sure they are likely to be approved by the senior executive or by the board. You won't want to get someone's hopes up and then have to say, "Sorry, but the pastor doesn't want you to serve."

4. Senior executive reviews candidates list.

5. Board reviews/approves candidates list.

6. Nominees invited to attend one or two board meetings.

who turns out to be a round peg in a square hole.

Remember to mark your trail during the selection process each time you go through it. That way you'll be able to combine your experience with the guidelines listed here, for even better results later on.

This guideline will help your nominating committee visualize the process for selecting a new member, even though your process may differ because of your organization's governmental form or bylaws.

2

---

7. Each nominee interviewed with spouse in nominee's home.

8. Nominee receives materials packet containing:

   a. Board Member Profile.

   b. Board Position Focus Sheet.

   c. The Selection Process outlined here.

   d. Leadership Commitment Agreement (see sample in the Appendix).

   e. "Ten Questions to Ask Before Deciding to Serve on the Board" (see list in the Appendix).

9. Nominee's references checked.

10. Final review conducted with senior executive, executive, committee, or entire board.

11. Board recommendation presented to deciding body.

12. Approval given.

13. Board extends official invitation.

14. New member signs Leadership Commitment Agreement.

15. New member begins orientation.

Section B
REFINING YOUR BOARD MEMBER PROFILE

**ESSENCE: *With no idea of diamonds,
we settle for glass.***

The Board Member Profile helps you describe what kind of person your board will look for in a new member.

Beyond a few ideal traits, too many boards have only a general idea ("a person with integrity") of what character

---

An "Ideal" Board Member Profile

- Meets Scriptural qualifications (1 Timothy 3, Titus 1).
- Has significant level of experience in situations that have demonstrated strong character qualities.
- Is God-oriented—with his life and sense of purpose focused more on God than on personal achievements, family, or a mission or program.
- Is motivated by faith in the supernatural work of God—a board-sized faith.
- Is a person of prayer.
- Is able to be decisive.
- Sees the Big Picture...has a worldwide perspective.
- Is positive and focused on the future, yet is also realistic—aware of reality, but not shackled by it.
- Wants to win, not just get by.
- Thinks critically, without a critical attitude.
- Is a natural encourager, a cheerleader for the whole group, including the senior executive and rest of board.
- Believes strongly in the objectives of the organization.
- Feels at ease in an advising relationship with the senior executive.
- "Fits" with current board members.

---

qualities and expertise they want in a board member. The clearer you and your board can be about your preferred candidate, the higher the likelihood of your finding him.

Below you'll see an "ideal" Board Member Profile (see also on page 38 the "Danger Signals" in a candidate profile). Again, be careful not to simply adopt this for your board's use. Rather, see it as a sample to adapt, although having this starting point should save you hours of work.

Having an ideal Board Member Profile becomes critical when you're considering two or three worthy candidates but you can only add one to the board. The clearer you can be in defining the specific qualifications you're looking for, the more obvious it will become which choice is best.

2

- Is not a "rubber stamp"—giving an automatic Yes; nor is he a "devil's advocate"—with an automatic No.
- Enjoys a wide network of friends and professional contacts.
- Can think independently without insisting on "my way."
- Is humble and not judgmental—gives priority to the "beam" in his own eye, not the "speck" in his brother's.
- Keeps priorities clear while being able to sort many details in a confusing situation.
- Shows a willingness to adapt a program to meet needs.
- Demonstrates ability to delegate effectively.
- Has a spouse willing to have him serve on the board.
- Presents no conflict of interests.
- Has a servant-leader attitude—"How can I help the group win?"
- Is willing to work, to do homework, to serve.
- Is able to work *with* the team, not against it.
- Brings a wide variety of successful experiences.
- Has rebounded from failure, with integrity.
- Demonstrates a commitment to honesty, loyalty, and excellence.
- Understands the importance of confidentiality on sensitive information.
- Shows a desire to grow and to learn.

Danger signals in a board candidate profile:

- Has personal (hidden) agendas.
- Is consistently negative, always focusing on why something can't be done.
- Is fearful of the future.
- Is stingy.
- Is extremely emotional, needy, or self-centered.

Section C
REFINING YOUR BOARD'S POSITION FOCUS SHEET

ESSENCE: Before you start looking for a peg, decide what hole you want to fill.

The Board Member Profile is primarily a description of the *kind of person* you're looking for. The Position Focus Sheet defines what that person will be expected to *do* as a board member.

Before you ask new members to serve on a board, be prepared to tell them exactly what is expected of them. A clear Position Focus Sheet (see the sample in the Appendix) helps avoid frustration and tension from wrong assumptions.

The Position Focus Sheet is similar to a job description. But a Position Focus Sheet differs in that it tries to limit to one sheet of paper the essential assumptions being made about a position without going into detail as to how the tasks will be accomplished.

SUMMARY

The three most important steps in selecting board members:

2

1. Understand the selection process.

2. Develop an ideal Board Member Profile so you know who you're looking for.

3. Develop a Position Focus Sheet so you know exactly what you want the new member to do.

Adapt these samples to your own use, mark your trail, and refine your process each time you use it.

YOU HAVE NOW concluded Chapter Two and Step 2 in the Board Process. Again, you may want to check off your progress on page 13 as you continue increasing your Boardroom Confidence.

The BOARD PROCESS Chart
For Boardroom Confidence

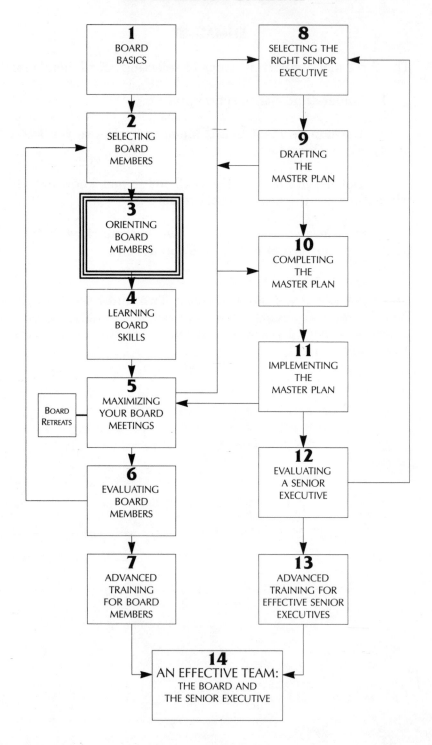

3

ORIENTING NEW MEMBERS

Essence: _In determining the depth and duration of a new board member's commitment, your first three sessions with that person are critical._

CONCENTRATE a good deal of energy on getting a new member started correctly. Both his future and yours depend on it. The member who feels welcome, accepted, and comfortable at his first few meetings will perform better, stay longer, and contribute more to your board.

Section A
THE FIRST INTERVIEW

Essence: _A person will accept or reject your proposal of his board service in the first ten minutes of your presentation._

IF INTERVIEWING board candidates becomes your responsibility, prepare particularly well for your first ten minutes of discussion. The prospective board member's view of the board—its organization, concerns, effectiveness—is actually shaped in that first few minutes. During that first interview, help him* see what his role and responsibilities would be, and begin orienting him to the values and perspective of the board.

Remember that one of the reasons people agree to serve on a board is the "need to feel needed" and wanted. After you explain the board selection process, tell him that the senior executive and the board have already approved your talking with him, and that they are excited about his interest (he'll feel wanted). Also, be able to explain the unique contribution you believe he'll make to the board (he'll feel needed).

Assuming the Nominating Committee has done its work and you are ready to ask this person to join the board...you may want to say something like: "I want you to know, Sam, that the senior executive and the board and I have all unanimously agreed that we *want* you to serve on our board. And because of your expertise in _____, you're *needed* on the board. I would like to invite you to become a member of the board of directors."

Often when an individual is deciding whether he wants to serve on a board, the "wanted/needed factor" is the delicate feather that tips the decision balance in favor of saying yes.

---

* The boards we have in mind as we write this book include both male and female members. But to avoid the awkward "he/she," "her/him" complexity that comes in trying to be "equal," we'll often be using the inclusive pronouns "he," "him" and "his" as referring to both genders.

Section B
MAKING NEW BOARD MEMBERS
FEEL WELCOME

*ESSENCE: Go out of your way to
make new members feel welcome.*

3

PEOPLE LIKE PEOPLE who welcome them. You'll always be remembered and appreciated by the new members you make feel welcome in their first session on the board.

A proper introduction is especially critical. DO IT RIGHT! How your new member feels about being on the board will be shaped in part by the quality of the introduction he receives to the board.

At the same time, the response to the new member by existing members—the anticipation, credibility, trust, and honor with which they view him—also depends on the introduction given in the new member's first session. Therefore, you and/or a member of the board should plan a proper introduction. You may find these suggestions helpful:

1. Prior to the meeting, ask the new member how he or she would like to be introduced. People often have definite preferences on this. Honor their requests.

2. Show the person's heart and character by telling about some actual encounter you've had with him. This could be a story or an illustration that would be meaningful to the board.

3. Deepen the board's appreciation for the person by recounting some of the person's accomplishments, his interest and desire to serve the organization, or any other information that would build his credibility with the board.

Here are other ways to make new members feel wanted and welcome:

1. Give them a reception with special refreshments. Even if your board normally has coffee and tea, this time have some cake or special refreshments that say, "This is an important occasion; we want to welcome our new friends."

2. Consider a news release announcing the new members' appointment to the board. Report their appointments in your in-house newsletter or other publication received by all members of your organization.

3. Arrange an informal question-and-answer session with the board to highlight their strengths, talents, and accomplishments. Ask questions like these:

    a. What have you done in your professional life that you're most proud of today?

    b. If you could be remembered for only one thing in life, what would it be?

    c. Why have you chosen to give of your valuable time and energy to serve on this board?

Do everything you can to see that new members appreciate and respect the board, and that the board appreciates and respects them. If you can accomplish this, you'll have made an outstanding investment in your board—an investment that will realize earnings in the future as the new members make significant contributions to the organization.

Section C
YOUR ORIENTATION CHECKLIST

Essence: Have a progressive, comprehensive plan to ensure that new members get off to the right start in the first weeks and months of board service. (In this, as in so many endeavors, checklists keep important things from slipping through the cracks.)

YOU ALREADY MAY HAVE a checklist for orienting new members to your board. If so, look over the checklist on the next page to see if there's anything you want to add to yours. If you don't have a checklist, use ours as a starting point and add items which are specific to your organization.

A checklist gives you a progressively comprehensive way to ensure that new members get off to the right start. Orientation of a new board member does not have to take a great deal of time. You simply have to make sure he has an understanding of the fundamentals of your board. This can happen over a lunch or two, or in an evening meeting.

Without a systematic orientation, a new board member may hold up board meetings simply because he is uninformed as to the way the board functions or what progress it has made. If you are going to ask someone to join your board, you owe it to him to clue him in, quickly and completely.

If, after reading this chapter, you see a significant omission in the approach your board takes to educating new members, why not volunteer to compile a more effective orientation checklist for them?

Orientation for New Members
A SAMPLE CHECKLIST

❑ Arrange for new members to have one-day retreat with senior executive.

❑ Take new group photo of board—copies signed (by all) and framed, and given to each new member.

❑ Ask new members to read *BOARDROOM CONFIDENCE.*

❑ Provide new members with overview:

1. *Where we've been*
   Group history if needed
   Minutes of the board (last six to twelve months)
   Financial summaries
   Questions and answers

2. *Where we are*
   Policy and procedures
   Current major projects update
   Board roster introduction (if needed)
   Organizational chart/staff introduction (if needed)
   Questions and answers

3. *Where we're going*
   Master Plan
   Annual planning calendar
   Questions and answers

❑ Present new members with any new assignments (if needed).

SUMMARY

The orientation of new board members begins with the first ten minutes of the initial interview. Making each new member feel welcome during his first few sessions will help him feel comfortable during his entire time on the board.

An orientation checklist keeps important things from being overlooked, and helps your board win the new member's respect and loyalty.

3

YOU'VE NOW finished Step 3 of the Board Process (be sure to check it off on page 13) as you continue building your board-room confidence.

The BOARD PROCESS Chart
For Boardroom Confidence

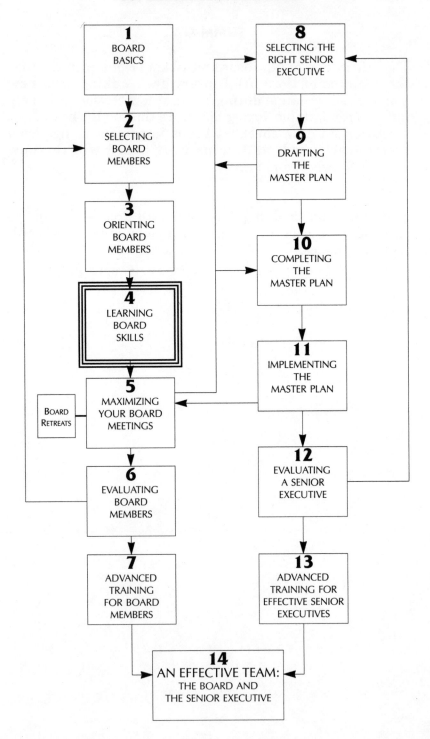

4

LEARNING BOARD SKILLS

**ESSENCE: Be quick to make or second motions for basic board training.**

As we work with many boards, we often hear members express anxiety because they have been asked to accept a responsibility without being prepared to succeed at it. They're afraid they will look bad, will make unwise decisions, will accept something that should be rejected, or will reject something that should be accepted.

What's needed is specific board skills training. Any member worth having on a board doesn't want to just sit quietly—watching and listening without initiating or contributing. Yet neither does he want to say or do the wrong thing out of ignorance.

Reading this book is probably more training than seventy percent of all board members ever receive. Is it any mystery so many feel so unprepared to serve?

With some basic training in boardsmanship and the fundamental skills of being an effective board member, you'll find some of your quieter members beginning to contribute their wisdom in a truly helpful way. Then you and the entire board will benefit by gaining the best input from every member, not just those who feel confident because of former board experience.

Section A
APPRECIATING, RECOGNIZING, AND ENCOURAGING

*ESSENCE: Appreciation is thanking,
Recognition is seeing,
and Encouragement is bringing hope
for the future.*

SPECIALIZE IN BEING an appreciator of every major contribution, a recognizer of every positive attitude or service, and an encourager to everyone. Everyone does better when he feels liked and appreciated, and he in turn appreciates those who give him genuine encouragement.

These three skills—appreciation, recognition, and encouragement—are among the most meaningful you have to offer your board In fact, every board should set aside a percentage of its income for appreciating, recognizing, and encouraging.

GIFTS OF APPRECIATION

> *"Every man is a friend to him
> who gives gifts."* (Proverbs 19:6)

It's amazing how much good will a board can create by giving a simple memento—a cup, a pen, a T-shirt—to commemorate a key event. This is especially true with foreign visitors from countries where gift-giving is expected. Typically, when a foreign visitor appears before a board, he brings a gift. Not anticipating this, frequently the board is left in the awkward position of having received a gift, but not being prepared to give one in return.

When a visitor appears before your board, see that someone on the board has prepared a gift of appreciation for his visit to your organization. (You don't need ten years of board experience to take this initiative.)

Another way of showing appreciation could be to offer gifts to shut-ins (invalids restricted to their homes) within your organization. Giving tapes of sermons or speeches, books, booklets, study guides, workbooks, notebooks—anything that would help fill their lonely hours—would be appropriate for the board to make available to shut-in members of your group.

Provide some financial flexibility (for example, a special benevolence fund) to allow the pastor or senior executive to give tapes, books, workbooks or cards to supporters in need.

AWARDS IN RECOGNITION OF CONTRIBUTION

Most of the time, the contribution you make to an organization as a board member is an intangible one. You don't create a book, build a building, or manufacture a product; rather, you give counsel, hours of time and discussion, and possibly inspiration.

The same is true of the senior executive, who may go for years at a time without his hand actually creating a tangible product. A senior pastor can spend five years preaching, counseling, inspiring, and leading—and at the end of the five years not have a single, tangible product that he has created. He can easily feel his contribution has evaporated. But one simple award expressing how significant his contribution has been, signed by all the members of the board, can make a major difference in his feeling of accomplishment.

Ideally, the mature Christian leader would not or should not need such tangible motivations. A plaque or other award to express appreciation for one's contribution may seem unnecessary. In reality, we're all delighted when others notice that we've made a significant difference.

Former members also deserve to be appreciated and recognized for their contribution. You may find that putting a picture of former boards in a hallway, or plaques naming former board members, would be a valuable historic gesture on the part of the board.

Offering recognition awards should not be limited to your group. Recognition can be one of those major areas of ag-

gressive ministry for your board. Consider giving community awards—Coach of the Year, Teacher of the Year, Citizen of
the Year. You may ask, "Is that the role of our church? I've
never heard of a church doing that." But if you were a community leader who demonstrated Christian values, you
would be impressed by a church that noticed. That one act
of recognition could be the beginning of a positive, influen-
tial relationship.

Note: When giving recognition to more than one person
at once, always list names alphabetically to avoid uninten-
tionally hurt feelings.

WORDS OR LETTERS OF ENCOURAGEMENT

Words of encouragement bring invaluable support and a
feeling of hope for the future. You will find your words of encouragement are often life-shaping, especially for young
leaders.

Can you imagine being a teen leader and getting a letter
in the mail—two or three paragraphs in length, and signed
by each board member—that clearly expressed recognition
and appreciation for your potential as a young leader? If
that would have encouraged you as a teenager...do unto
others as you'd have them do unto you.

Recently a young friend shared that just a few words of
encouragement over a two- or three-year period had given
him courage in situations where he had never felt comfortable or confident in the past. He said only one person had
been an encourager in his life, but this person's encouragement had changed his life.

Remember, one thoughtful letter from your board affirm-
ing a person's ability and worth to the organization can
change his—and your—future for the better.

Appreciating, recognizing and encouraging are three of
the board's most valuable contributions. Specialize in these
three skills, and even if you do nothing else, you will have
made a significant contribution.

Section B
BRAINSTORMING

ESSENCE: *A brainstorming session is to a designer what a home-cooked meal is to a hungry hobo.*

4B

IN BRAINSTORMING SESSIONS, completely abandon the constraints of "reality" and help others do the same. If you're the kind of person who prefers sticking to the norm in your day-to-day thinking, you may find brainstorming sessions a source of anxiety.

If that's true for you, may we suggest you imagine two hats on a hat rack. One is a "blue-sky" hat where there are no limits on possibilities. The other is a "reality" hat, where the "cold, hard facts" decide what does or does not happen. In a brainstorming session, imagine yourself walking over to the hat rack, taking off your "reality" hat and putting on your "blue-sky" hat. Once the brainstorming session has been completed, walk over to the hat rack and put on your "reality" hat. Then take a look at all the brilliant new ideas which have come to you and select the ones you should try to help become reality. (If, during the brainstorming session, you see another member struggling or feeling anxious, encourage him to go to the same hat rack.)

Come to brainstorming sessions looking for the breakthrough ideas, the brilliant ideas that will make a major long-term difference. The person who deals only in reality completely overlooks the possibility of a breakthrough idea. Take the risk that a new idea might set your organization on a path to solving a baffling problem or developing a new, significant ministry. There is plenty of time for reality later.

NOTHING IS MEANINGFUL WITHOUT A CONTEXT.

When you change the context in any discussion, new options become obvious. Imagine for a minute that your annual budget of $500,000 is now $5,000,000. Immediately the context changes. The context for every problem you're dealing with is changed. You see new options you never saw when you were limiting yourself to the smaller budget.

That is why brainstorming is such an extremely valuable tool for you as a board member. While you're sitting in a board meeting, even though it is not a brainstorming session, if you want to get a different perspective on a problem, ask yourself some brainstorming questions (see the list in the Appendix).

Dreaming of what *could be* in the future opens up new options, bringing hope to all but the fearful. Since most positive motivation has to do with the future, new ideas act like powerful magnets, pulling you into the future.

A team forms around a dream. No dream, no team. Good people won't stay with your organization if it has no clear dream. And often the dream part of the organization comes not as a result of logical, "realistic" planning, but as a result of brainstorming, when you see possibilities you've never before considered.

We have been taught all our lives that time is money, and so it is. But ideas are also worth money. Many ideas are worth millions the minute they're born.

One idea we developed together at World Vision was the Love Loaf program. What was this idea worth the first day it was imagined? We weren't sure—then. Now we know. The Love Loaf program has raised in excess of $50,000,000. Sorting out which ideas are worth pursuing takes time and experience. Brainstorming is like mining for ideas—ideas that could be diamonds.

You may ask, "If ideas are so valuable, why are brainstorming sessions so threatening?" Brainstorming is threatening because ideas represent change, and all change represents loss of some kind. For people who are fearful, the idea of change represents great threat. The subject of change will be covered more completely in the next section.

To help you develop good brainstorming skills, we've included on the next page a list of eight guidelines that serve as an adaptable introduction for your brainstorming sessions.

Eight Guidelines for Our Brainstorming Session

1. Our dreams in life will be limited by the size of the need we allow ourselves to see. Let's focus on needs we see and let our ideas (possible solutions for the needs) flow freely.

2. It is very acceptable not to enjoy brainstorming—not everyone does. But in a special session like this, let's consider ideas regardless of how unlikely they may seem today.

3. Let's listen to what is right, not who is right. The dreamer who can't implement his own idea may still have the best idea. Someone else can be asked later to make it work.

4. We'll ask Brainstorming Questions (see the list in the Appendix) when we get stale in our mental stretching.

5. Let's keep track of who has what ideas. Ideas are as real to an idea person as a product is to a craftsman. Failing to give proper recognition to a person for his idea is like stealing something out of his hand. To ensure proper recognition, each of us will have a stack of 3-by-5 cards, and will write each of our ideas on a card with our name or initials on it. This way we can keep track of who had the ideas that turned out to be the real winners.

6. In this session, let's agree to allow no negative comments. For now, the more ideas the better...regardless of how practical or impractical each may seem at the time.

7. In this session we will concentrate on the subject of _____ and the session will be _____ minutes long.

8. At the end of the session we'll sort out the best ideas (using the Idea Sorter Questions in the Appendix).

4B

Section C
CHANGING

ESSENCE: *All change represents loss of some kind; that's why some of us resist it so strongly.*

MASTER THE ART of presenting changes to your group in a way that results in rejoicing, not resistance. You can rarely eliminate all resistance to change, but you can drastically reduce resistance by proper planning and presentation.

(NOTE: *Changes in plans or procedures are the result of one or more basic decisions. As you anticipate such a change, you may want to review briefly the Decision Making Questions listed in the Appendix. These can help you double-check your logic prior to announcing any change.)*

WHY PEOPLE RESIST CHANGE

Most resistance to change comes from fear of loss. People need to be reassured that within the new program, the new plan, the new way, they will have a niche. They need to see what that niche will be before they can feel comfortable with the coming change. The primary question you must answer for them is, "What will this change actually mean to me on a day-to-day basis?"

With major change, people often sense a loss of control, and indecision about what to do or what will happen next. That is why change is so stressful for most of us.

Here are three questions to help any of us know if we are overreacting to a "forced" change:

1. Am I tired, sick, or upset at home or at work? If you are tired or sick you will tend to be negative; if you are upset at work or home you will tend to bring your emotional turmoil to the group's decision-making process. Beware! If you find yourself resisting

change for these reasons, try to listen to your head instead of your emotions.

2. Does the change involve something I feel is illegal, immoral, or unethical? If you believe strongly that this is so, resist it—period.

3. What difference will it really make? If you feel a change is going to make a drastic, negative difference, then resist it. But if you can say, "It really doesn't matter; it's just my personal preference," then relax and cooperate with someone else's idea.

PROCESS FOR MAKING CHANGE EASIER

Carefully thinking through the proposed changes and their implications will greatly increase your ability to convince the most resistant board member. The following points will help you refine your presentations.

1. *Timing is critical.*

Introduce change when those affected are refreshed, not fatigued. The great football coach Vince Lombardi drilled this message into his players' thinking: "Fatigue makes cowards of us all." Fatigue makes even small changes seem overwhelming; it turns us introspective and negative.

Second, make sure the change is perceived as meeting one of their (not *your*) current needs. When you can show others in the organization that they've had a need for a long time which can now be met by this change, they'll tend to rejoice rather than resist.

Third, consider making what some organizations call "block changes." People can fairly easily absorb a major change in their work environment about once a year. It's far more unsettling to continue making small changes daily or weekly. Although small, intermittent change may seem preferable to you, you may want to wait and make all your changes at once—especially if you expect resistance.

2. *Make changes that make sense.*

When introducing change, your presentation should cover five basic areas, related to the five basic phases in which new ideas are developed and perceived. These five phases in the development of an idea are: the *design* phase, the *design/develop* phase, the *develop* phase, the *develop/manage* phase, and the *manage* phase.

We've found that in interacting with a new idea, each person tends to prefer one of the five phases. This same preference seems to govern the way that person responds typically to change. Understanding these various role preferences and typical responses will therefore help you when introducing change.

Whenever change is introduced...

- the *designer* looks for the theoretical framework of the new change.
- the *designer/developer* looks for the process of the change (the next five to ten steps).
- the *developer* looks for the new goal in the change.
- the *developer/manager* looks at how it will improve results.
- the *manager* looks at how the change can be controlled.

It's good strategy, therefore, to explain change in terms that address the concerns of each of the five role orientations. First, explain the theory of your change, then the process (the next ten steps, for example) of your change, then the goal of the change, then the expected results of the change, and finally, how you're going to control the change so it doesn't get out of hand.

As you present these perspectives on change, each person can relax and feel that his or her questions have been addressed.

Be careful to show that you are aware of any road blocks to the proposed change. As you present your plan for dealing with these roadblocks, your listeners will know you've done your homework.

3. *Explaining "why" is not mandatory, but it makes accepting change much easier.*

Reasonable change is rarely resisted. People do what makes sense to them. It is unreasonable change that upsets people. As a board member who is introducing some change to the organization, you should emphasize the need that the change is meeting.

Dramatization of your point is a persuasive way to win support. Assume you decide to introduce new padded pews into the sanctuary at church. The old pews had not been padded and you are proposing that funds be approved for new pews with padding. You may want to have everyone come into the old sanctuary and sit on the unpadded pews for a two-hour discussion. After everyone is tired of sitting without pads, explain why you feel it is wise to order padded pews. The resistance would certainly be less! Always present your new idea as a response to their needs, not your own.

4c

Another winning strategy is to project today's pressing need to its logical conclusion. Project a trend line showing what "might be" in a year or two. Paint word pictures that show how risky it is to allow the need to grow two or three times as acute as it is today.

Admit that if needs don't escalate, there would be no justifiable reason to change. But if you can demonstrate the likelihood of increased pressure, greater demand, higher volume, or more people—a change will seem reasonable. After all, a leader's job is to anticipate tomorrow's needs today, while your organization has time to make well-thought-out changes.

One final suggestion: Make specific notes on how change is typically presented, processed and resisted in your organization. The more you can help people accept change, the more effective will be your leadership as a board member.

Section D
COMMITTEES

_**ESSENCE**: A committee is like a match—
used properly, beautiful things happen; used wrongly,
the result is tragedy._

COMMITTEES SAVE the whole board long hours of inefficient discussion. Members assigned to a committee whose concern is something they have personal interest in will accomplish much more than a whole board that is mostly disinterested. See your committee assignments, then, not as a prison sentence, but as advanced leadership training for you personally and a timesaver for the board as a whole.

One predictable problem arises from a committee structure in a small growing organization, and especially a small church. The problem develops like this: In order to reduce risk and divide the labor, the board establishes standing committees (for example, a Christian education committee) in the absence of professional staff. But as the church grows and adds professional staff (a Christian education director, for instance), the board often errs by keeping the committees. Almost inevitably a conflict of authority arises. To whom does the staff person report—the committee, or the senior executive?

In our opinion, the minute you add a full-time professional staff member, the board should disband the committee that oversaw the area now led by the new staff person. This does not remove lay people from input, but it does provide for a clearer line of authority.

We've identified four keys to making committees effective:

1. _Choose the right people._ Select people who _want_ to serve on a given committee. They will be the most productive because they have a personal interest. Consider not only their interest, but also their expertise and experience. Also, it helps to place on a com-

mittee those people who work well together, with complementary abilities.

2. *Establish clear expectations.* The board needs to clearly communicate what it expects the committee to accomplish. Providing specific objectives allows the committee (and the board) to monitor progress and measure success. If funding is involved, indicate the amount budgeted.

4D

3. *Set a length of term for committee membership.* If a person serves on the same committee too long, he will become discouraged, unproductive, or both. Set a reasonable term length for all committee assignments.

4. *Give the committee deadlines.* Most committees will achieve more, in a shorter time, if they are given a specific time limit to complete their task.

When a committee is ready to report back to the board, one person should be assigned to write the first draft of the report. Committees don't create well, but they can effectively review and refine the report for final presentation.

Section E
COMMUNICATING

ESSENCE: Communication is an organization's lifeblood.

OF ALL THE FRUSTRATIONS we've heard expressed in organizations during the past thirty years, one of the most frequent is a lack of communication. Hundreds of consultants have emerged to help groups learn to communicate more effectively with their constituents, staffs, and boards.

Every investment your board makes in improving communication will strengthen the organization.

Here are some practical suggestions:

1. *Practice good listening skills.*

Listen to peeps, squeaks, squawks and screams. Train yourself to listen with more than ears, to hear more than words. Listen to the feelings, implications, assumptions and possibilities underlying the words. As you develop your listening skills, you will begin hearing more accurately what the person is really saying to you.

Listen carefully to the individual expressing complaints or frustrations. That one person may represent fifteen people who didn't come to you, but would bring the same message if they did. You need wisdom to discern which of the complaints or negative reports you're hearing represent just the reporter's concern, and which in fact represent the concerns of others, too.

Listen carefully for heart motives. Psychologist James Dobson often says, "Ask not only what a person does, but why he does it." Occasionally you will see a person do something completely out of character. They may act, react or say something you never expected them to say. When this happens, ask yourself: "Did they have an argument at home? Are they depressed in business? Do they have a hidden agenda? Why did they say what they said?"

Monitor how you're handling your personal life. We all have unmet needs. We all have concerns and pressures at home and work which have the potential of reducing our boardroom effectiveness. We can't avoid distress and even crises in our personal lives, but it is a mistake to make recommendations for the organization based on the disruption in our own affairs. Be aware of your own emotional needs. Make sure the counsel you're giving is based on clear, objective insight.

2. *Develop a "You Focus" style of communication.*

4E

Having a "You Focus" means looking at everything you're trying to communicate from the other person's perspective rather than your own. (This is explained in more detail in a tape series called *You Focus,* available from Masterplanning Group International.)

Ask yourself, "If I were him, what would be my reaction?" Then, "Do unto others as you would have them do unto you." Talk to each person in your audience the way you would want to be talked to if you were in their position. Be as considerate of the person to whom you're speaking as you would want a speaker to be of you.

This "You-Focus" style of communication applies to everything from board articles in the bulletin, to annual reports; from a building marquee, to slogans and themes...it applies everywhere. As a board member, pay special attention to what is being communicated from your organization. It is important that your organizational communication be serving, not self-centered.

3. *Avoid negative communication.*

Knowing what goes wrong with communication is nearly as important as knowing what makes it go right.

The most common culprit for communication foul-ups is wrong assumptions. Whenever you find frustration and tension within the board or between the board and others—the senior executive, the organization's staff, or the community—go back to spelling out assumptions.

You can be a great peacemaker if you simply identify differing assumptions, discuss them to the point of agreement, then build together on your common understanding.

Using a policy and procedure manual can be a big help in achieving clear communication. Having policies and procedures simply and clearly stated precludes many common assumption errors. (Remember, policy is what we always do or never do, while procedures are the how-to steps for carrying it out. The clearer your policy and procedure statements, the better your chances of clear and positive communication.)

4. *Don't confront. Clarify!*

Sometimes in the process of discussing an issue with a fellow board member, you suddenly get that uneasy feeling which warns, "We are now in an argument." When that happens, follow these steps:

a. Relax. Settle back in your chair and take a deep breath.

b. Put the issue on paper.

c. Say to the person, "I'd like to clarify some elements of the issue we're discussing." Begin to write these out rather than continuing to talk about them directly and personally. By shifting the attention to the written form, you objectify the problem and keep it from becoming a personal confrontation.

d. In your mind, switch from the word *confront* ("I'm in a confrontation")...to the word *clarification* ("We're in the process of clarifying this issue").

e. Look for ways you can agree with the other person's view without compromising your own.

f. Say: "You know, Sam, we're on the same side of the struggle here. We're not enemies, we're friends. The problem is the enemy."

Clarify the issue rather than confront the person. Spell out the assumptions rather than take things personally. You will find your heart rate dropping, your peace of mind returning, and your love for the person remaining intact.

One additional thought: Whenever a hostile confrontation starts between board members,
you might suggest a refreshment break. Let emotions calm. While others are drinking their coffee, list the assumptions you hear on both sides of the issue, and try to sort out where the parties are miscommunicating. This is a helpful, peacemaking role you can play on the board, even in your first board session.

4E

5. *Make in-house communication a high priority.*

Frustration between the board and staff is a frequent concern. Yet most internal communication problems in an organization result from one broad problem—there is no clear organizational chart, no clear chain of command, and therefore no practical reporting process. Staff members feel left out and in the dark.

If this is true in your organization, press for an organizational chart and good reporting system (see Chapter Eleven).

Develop and use a distribution list for information. This list should show all the people at various levels in the organization who should get certain information. For example, whenever a new policy is established, check the list to make sure a statement goes to the right people at the right time.

6. *Communicate regularly with your constituency.*

For a board to have proper presence, authority and influence among its constituents, these people must hear from the board regularly. A seen-but-never-heard board (or, worse, a never-seen-and-never-heard board) has little influence and is forfeiting much of its power.

One of the main communications channels within any organization is its newsletter. A regular board presence in the newsletter gives the board visibility and credibility in the eyes of constituents.

Another way to build board visibility, especially in a local church, is to have open forums. The elders of the Fresno (California) Evangelical Free Church occasionally hand out 3-by-5 cards on Sunday morning and ask members to write out any question they may want to ask the board. Later, on a Sunday evening, the board sits on the platform, panel-style, and answers these questions.

Even though the majority may not attend such a session, the nonverbal communication to the entire church is that the board is open to input from everyone. A forum is also an opportunity for constituents to get to know the board, to see the board as real people who have heartfelt concerns for the church. It is a positive, major communication opportunity that shouldn't be overlooked.

Public presentations of appreciation and recognition can greatly enhance your board's effectiveness. These events give you a chance to convey your values to the entire group in a positive setting.

7. *Communicate regularly with the public.*

Whenever there is community exposure to the board or to your group, you want to give the best impression. You will best serve the board and the organization if you have a board-appointed spokesman who is respected in the community, articulate, and intimately informed on all the issues with which you deal.

You may also want to appoint one person to specialize in getting media coverage for special key events organized by your group. This could be a board member, staff member, or one of your constituents. Often newsworthy developments that warrant media coverage go unreported because no one in the organization feels it is his or her responsibility to arrange such coverage.

Another key to productive community relations is to have a V.I.P. list for invitations to major events within your organization. Any time you have an open house, a building dedication, or major announcement, community leaders need to be invited.

Section F
DECISION MAKING

ESSENCE: *"You can please some of the people some of the time; you can please all of the people some of the time; but you can never please all the people all the time" (Abraham Lincoln).*

4F

YOU MUST BE ABLE to live with the fact that you're not going to please everyone all the time. That's part of being a leader.

You won't be right all the time, either. Yet wisdom in decision making is fundamental for a board member. Your responsibility is to continually improve in making wise choices.

Following are proven, practical strategies in a variety of areas for making the right decisions.

1. *Buy short.*

One way to limit your risk is to "buy short." An inexperienced leader will tend to order far too many pieces of a promotional brochure, for example, because the per-unit cost is much less. What he fails to see is that the actual dollars involved—and the risk to the organization—are far greater with the larger order. To the extent that you don't know what kind of financial return to expect from the brochure, it is often wiser to decide on a smaller initial order. Even if you have to reprint at a greater per-unit cost, the *risk* is far less.

2. *Put every choice in its proper context.*

Always ask, "What is the context that gives this decision meaning?" Three main contextualizing tools must be applied by boards:

a. The *goals statement* which gives you the directional context of the organization.

b. The *organizational chart* which helps you place your people within the context of the organization and identify the impact of your decision on each person.

c. The *financial reports* which tell you what's possible, and let you see what the dollar impact (and risk) could be.

In short, ask yourself, "What affect will this have on our direction, our people, and our financial position?"

3. *Understand how control points work.*

Every organization has five key control points. Being aware of them will help you retain and exercise appropriate authority. These control points are:

a. *direction*
b. *personnel*
c. *money*
d. *information*
e. *development and training*

Know who is in charge of these five areas. Is it the board, the senior executive, the executive staff? What percentage of control should each have? Without an understanding of the critical nature of these five control points, any board can make unwise decisions.

4. *Develop a crisis checklist.*

A crisis checklist is a necessity for each member of the board (see the sample in the Appendix). This is a plan you can implement immediately if something goes drastically wrong.

Play the "what if" game for an hour or two. What if our building caught fire? What if we were sued for a million dollars? What if some other major catastrophe happened?

Don't spend all your time worrying about things that will probably never happen. But, you may want to occasionally play this game to identify your vulnerabilities as an organization. This strategy becomes your "ounce of prevention."

5. *Get the facts.*

As Dr. Peter Drucker declares, "Once the facts are clear, the decisions jump out at you." One of the most frequent mistakes inexperienced leaders make is trying to decide before they know all the facts. It's like trying to decide whether to buy a Chevrolet or Cadillac when you don't know how much money you have in the bank.

A high percentage of your success as a board member comes from simply doing your homework: Do the research, get the facts, ask questions, conduct surveys, take field trips, set up trend lines (projections versus actuals) and compile multi-year comparisons. As the facts become clearer, you'll indeed see the right decisions "jump out at you."

It is also true that when the facts change, so do the decisions. A decision made wisely today may need to be reversed a month from now when the facts change.

6. *Know when to say no.*

One of the frequent anxieties of board work is knowing when to go along with the group and when to say, "Absolutely not." Obviously, whenever something is undoubtedly illegal, immoral, or unethical, plant your feet like a mule—don't even negotiate. But when the issue is one of preference, method or procedure, and you can't convince the group of your perspective within a relatively short period of time, we suggest you "go with the flow." The way you prefer to do something may not be much better than someone else's idea. In any case, it probably isn't enough better to waste the group's time debating the issue.

Another rule of thumb: Whenever the board is about to make a reversible decision, a decision that you could change in the next meeting if you cared to, go with the flow. But when you're about to make a hard-to-change decision that would have impact for years to come, make decisions slowly and encourage the group to do the same. For example, there

69

is a major difference between deciding how to allocate a small percentage of some budget account versus deciding who to select as the organization's senior executive.

In summary: Whenever possible, agree with the group. If you feel something is unwise or nearly irreversible, ask questions until you're sure the issues are clear to you and to everyone. And when you're sure the considered decision is illegal, immoral, or unethical, say no immediately.

7. *Review your questions checklist before any major decision.*

When forced to make a major decision quickly, always review a checklist of questions. (You may want to use three lists in the Appendix—Brainstorming Questions, Decision Making Questions, and Idea Sorter Questions—as a basis for creating your own list of questions.)

8. *Draw up a timeline with "go/no-go" points.*

One way to reduce your decision-making risk is to set up a timeline with "go/no-go" points in the future. For example: "In phase one—from September to November—we will spend $10,000, then evaluate the program before spending any more. In December we will decide whether or not to proceed to the second phase, from January to April, which is budgeted at $40,000. At the beginning of May, after the end of phase two, we will make the decision whether to commit the final $100,000 for phase three in June and July." This limits your risk to one phase at a time.

9. *Hold out for unanimous agreement.*

One question boards frequently ask us is, "Should our group operate on a majority vote or insist on and wait for unanimous agreement?" If your board has been discussing this, maybe some outside perspective would be helpful.

We have found not only that unanimous agreement is possible, but that it is actually common among the boards with which we have worked.

We encourage your board to decide as a group to work through any issue until a certain decision "just makes sense" to everyone.

Having one "squeaky wheel" that simply won't get in line and agree with everyone else can be very frustrating. But at the same time, after hours of discussion, you may find that the one squeaky wheel was right all along. It may have been the only time that wheel has squeaked for months, but it could lead you to very wise and protective decision. If you had gone with the majority vote of the group, you may have made a very unwise move.

4F

If you come to an impasse on a subject, table it until the next meeting. Then bring it back up and see if changes have occurred that could clarify the issue.

If two board members are in sharp disagreement, they may want to have lunch together and talk the issue out without taking the entire board's time to do so. Another advantage of having two people discuss a disagreement in private is that no "face saving" has to be done later.

You will find both personal energy and group energy generated as you discuss something to the point of unanimous agreement. Through discussion, reason, prayer, understanding and cooperation—all the things that go into group dynamics—your group should arrive naturally to the point of 100-percent agreement (without anyone being pressured into agreement).

A warning note: The above discussion assumes that your board consists of reasonable, balanced, mature individuals. One person who is not can keep a board tied up for years, which is why the board selection process is so crucial.

10. *Develop worst- and best-case scenarios.*

Paul Schultheis, president of Real Properties, Inc., says this about risk: "Until you know the worst possible thing that could happen and the best possible thing that could happen, your risk equation is incomplete." Look carefully at what might happen both negatively and positively. An inexperienced leader will tend to look only at the worst or the best that could happen, and not consider the opposite for balance.

Section G
FUND RAISING

**ESSENCE: If you raise enough dollars,
budget is never a problem;
if you don't, it always is.**

WHEN IT COMES to generating dollars, there are four fundamental ways to do it:

1. Earn it.
2. Ask for it.
3. Borrow it.
4. Sell something.

We will concentrate our attention in this section on
asking for dollars, since that is the primary means of con-
ventional fund raising. Paul Schultheis advises, "You should
not only ask 'Can we afford it,' but 'How can we afford it?'"
Clarify your dream, then think creatively about how to
generate enough dollars to achieve the dream.

Let your dreams pull you into the future rather than automatically allowing the budget be your box. If you plan
based only on what you *have*, you will never grow beyond
what you are. Don't be guilty of the kind of thinking which
says, "We only have two dollars, therefore we can only have
two dollars worth of ministry or service."

The following list of components of successful fund
raising can help you approach it confidently and wisely:

1. *The name list is the foundation of fund raising.*

Nearly every fund-raising strategy is based on a list of
people to whom you can appeal for funds. In a church it is
the congregational directory; in a nonprofit organization it's
the mailing list.

One of the keys in generating a productive list is to

regard each person on the list as more than just a donor. Consider your list as 5,000 friends or team members.

In maintaining your list, track these four criteria:

a. The Source Code shows the original source of the name—how you first came in contact with it.

b. The Motivation Code identifies the specific appeal to which a person responded.

c. The Designation Code tells where the person would like his money applied.

d. The Mail Code designates what kind of mailings this person should receive.

4G

As we discussed in Chapter One, the service within an organization is always limited by the size of the resource base. It takes no genius to see, if you have 10 people who could give you $10 a month versus 1000 people who could give you $10 a month, you have an incredible difference in your ability to generate dollars and to provide service. If everyone responded to your request in the first case, you'd get $100 a month. In the other case you'd get $10,000. The larger your list, the larger your resource base and the larger your potential for providing significant service.

2. *Direct mail is the bread-and-butter way of asking.*

For a nonprofit organization, your bread-and-butter fund-raising approach is a regular mail appeal.

This needs to be done monthly. People tend to get paid, and to give, on a monthly basis rather than annually, quarterly or seasonally. When they get paid is when they are most likely to be able to give as much as they would like.

The most cost-effective way to communicate with your supporters regularly is through the mail. A good return ratio for a direct-mail appeal would be a 1-to-5 return...for every dollar you put into the direct mail program you get $5 in return. Of course, not every appeal will be equally successful.

Some appeals may return 1-to-10, others 1-to-3, and others may actually cost more than they generate. But on an annual basis your average return should be about 1-to-5.

One effective strategy is to rent names from other organizations' lists. These names often can be selected on an "nth" name basis for a test mailing—that is, every fifth or tenth or twenty-fifth name on the entire list gets an appeal on a test basis. Even if that test returns 1-to-10, resist the temptation to rent the entire list (of perhaps a million names) and send your appeal to all of them. This could be a financial disaster.

It's wiser to test once more, this time with just a few thousands of names. If that works, test again with a few more thousand names. If this test mailing pulls just as well, rent the entire list.

When you rent a list, don't expect the return ratio for it to be nearly as high as it is for your own "in-house" list. The main advantage of renting new names is that you acquire new donors, broadening your resource base.

3. *Charts help you track the right variables.*

In any fund-raising effort, you need to keep only a handful of charts to follow the big picture. A few examples:

a. Projected Income versus Actual Income
b. Projected Expense versus Actual Expense
c. Projected Net versus Actual Net
d. Percentage of Variance in Projected and Actual Income, Expense and Net

4. *A board opens doors and sets the example.*

One of the frequent misconceptions of a board is that board member are fund-raising machines. While we find many board members willing to be fund raisers, typically most are not. They don't know how to ask for money. Most board members should be seen as door-openers, not askers.

Another role board members can and should play in fund

raising is to donate money personally. Only a small percentage of the boards we have worked with have really wealthy
people as members. But you as a board member can be a
pace-setter in funding campaigns.

One final note: No matter how a board responds to the
challenge of generating dollars, it should not be seen as a re-
placement for the organization's fund-raising department.

5. *Cultivation is the key to repeat donations.*

4G

"People give to people" is a general rule. Your funding
appeals will be successful to the extent that you cultivate relationships with people through personal contact, reports
and frequent communications. Ask the staff to set up a
program of regular communications. Help each donor feel
part of the team just as though he or she were on staff. And,
always remember to say "Thank you!"

6. *An outside agency can increase team power.*

There are a number of advantages to working with an
outside agency in fund-raising programs. They can provide:

a. objectivity in discovering what is appealing within
   your organization.

b. public relations skills for creating effective written or
   visual appeals.

c. temporary staff you can pay on a per-diem or part-
   time basis.

d. professionals bringing an experience level that the
   typical staff person might not have.

In selecting an outside firm, consider the following:

a. Check the firm's success record with other groups
   similar to your own.

b. Note the personal chemistry between the account executives and your top leadership team, and especially the dynamics between your senior executive and the agency president.

c. Give an agency a small assignment to see how they do. For example, you may want to ask an agency to do a development audit to get an outsider's view of your current fund-raising activity. If they succeed, give them a larger test, and if they succeed again, they are good candidates for an exclusive working agreement.

7. *Building campaigns can attract "new" funds.*

Some wallets, safes, and purses stay locked—until you announce building plans. People who never respond to a regular, monthly appeal will enjoy being part of a building campaign.

When it comes to capital funds, you may want to seriously consider an outside agency. Their experience will often save you time, energy and money. One rule in capital funds campaigns is that an organization can typically raise in pledges (to be given over a period of three years) three times its annual budget.

Another capital funds guide: The success formula for attracting large gifts from corporations and foundations consists of about one-third research, one-third persistence, and one-third who-you-know.

8. *Good bank relations provide funding options.*

One key to effective banking relations is keeping accurate and timely accounts and reports going to your banker. "Keep the burner warm" even when you don't need to borrow money. A regular update of your financial status to the banker will be helpful when you do need a loan.

Occasionally you may need to set up a line of credit

based on historic seasonal ups and downs in your income. If
the pattern reoccurs year after year, you may want to set up
a credit line to borrow money during the low points, and
repay it during high-income months. Ideally, you should set
up a savings account during your high points to pay your
bills during the following low times.

9. *People usually give money for predictable reasons.*

4G

People give to churches and nonprofit organizations for
many reasons, but some of the most common are these:

    a. to tithe
    b. to reach a dream
    c. to meet a (personal or corporate) need
    d. tax considerations
    e. a generous spirit
    f. they've been asked by a friend
    g. to make a difference
    h. to memorialize a loved one
    i. to be recognized

Section H
GROUP DYNAMICS

ESSENCE: *"Before you can convince a man of anything, you must convince him you are his true friend" (Abraham Lincoln).*

MASTER THE ART of making friends—98 percent of your success on the board depends on it! Once everyone on the board is your true friend, your comments will make sense to them, and your motions will be seconded more quickly.

You'll find as you take proper time for social relationships, your meetings will actually end sooner. Often the refreshments at a board meeting are seen as a luxury rather than a necessity. Refreshments are, in fact, a part of the basic dynamics of a successful board meeting. At the refreshment break people tend to renew friendships. Positive relationships developed in the social part of the meeting allow more freedom of discussion in the business part.

Study the five group dynamics suggested here as you continue gaining boardroom confidence:

1. *Effective group dynamics don't happen by chance.*

In his book *The Effective Board*, Cyril Houle draws on twenty-five years of research to identify the essential principles of good group dynamics. His principles (we've listed them here at the end of Section H) are a good standard to strive for with your board.

2. *Personal agendas lead to anger and a need for control.*

When a board member is experiencing tremendous pressure in his personal or work relationships, he may show his stress in unusual ways. For example, a usually prudent board member who is on the point of personal bankruptcy may unexpectedly begin taking risky or difficult stands on board issues. If you are aware of what is going on the lives of the board members, you will be able to properly interpret any such lack of balance that any of them are exhibiting.

Another example of a personal agenda relates to differences in age and life interests. A church composed largely of people in or near their retirement years may find it difficult to see the need for new church facilities. These people may have built churches as young men and women, but because of the different phase of life they now are in, they may not be interested in responding to this kind of objective need any longer.

4H

Another factor is that health drastically affects a person's wisdom and objectivity. A severe cold, flu, or other illness reduces energy and mental alertness.

Be aware also of how jet lag can impair a person's thinking and perception. Be careful in accepting the counsel of the board member who has just flown in across three time zones.

3. *Frustration and tension come from differing assumptions.*

People in group situations tend to miscommunicate when they hold differing assumptions. That is why it is critical for every board member to agree on these basic items: the Master Plan; policy manual; Position Focus Sheets with separate and clear assignments; who is the directional leader; and who has final authority. You'll find the frustration and tension in the room drastically reduced as you learn to work from the same clear assumptions.

4. *You can't risk tuning out quieter board members.*

It's easy in the press of usual board discussions to ignore the hesitant or infrequent contribution of the quieter board member. Don't! If you do ignore those shy "squeaks," beware of the following hazards:

    a. You will often hurt the quieter member, who had ventured far from of his comfort zone to "squeak up."

He may resent other board members who continue to ramrod through the agenda without accepting his quiet contribution.

b. You may miss counsel that could change the group's direction for the better. The person who is often silent may be observing a land mine everyone else has missed.

c. You will damage or even destroy the board's morale. When any member is not seen as equal and respected by the group—as is often the case when the "steam-roller" effect is overpowering the quieter member in his presentation—it ultimately causes the whole group to think less of itself.

The counsel of any board member must be judged not on delivery, volume, or the personality of the speaker, but on its own merit.

5. *A tired board makes poor choices.*

Remember Vince Lombardi's statement: "Fatigue makes cowards of us all." Fatigue makes cowards—and fools—of boards. In the last minutes of a late-night agenda, boards will tend to make quick decisions they later come to regret. Moreover, you can predict a tired board will become touchy and argumentative. Whenever possible, make major decisions when the board is fresh and alert. If you see your board becoming tired, suggest a break or adjournment. You will avoid many unwise decisions.

Essential Principles
for Good Group Dynamics
from THE EFFECTIVE BOARD
by Cyril Houle

a.   Every board member accepts every other board member with due appreciation for his strengths and a tolerance of his quirks and weaknesses.

b.   There is an easy familiarity of approach among the members of the board with an awareness of one another's backgrounds and viewpoints.

c.   Everyone concerned with a particular decision actually helps to make it.

d.   The contribution of each person or group is recognized.

e.   The board has a sense of being rooted in some important tradition and of providing continuity for a program which has been and continues to be of importance.

f.   The whole attitude of the board is forward-looking, and there is a confident expectation of growth and development in the program.

g.   There is a clear definition of responsibilities so that each person knows what is expected of him.

h.   The members of the board can communicate easily with one another.

i.   There is a sense that the whole board is more important than any of its parts.

j.   There is a capacity to resolve dissent and discord or, if it cannot be resolved, to keep it in perspective in terms of larger purposes.

k.   There is acceptance of and conformity to a code of behavior, usually involving courtesy, self-discipline, and responsibility.

l.   There is an awareness of the fact that all boards contain clusters or pairs of persons who tend to like or dislike one

(continued on next page)

another, as well as some who may not be closely involved with others; but there is also a capacity to use these personal relationships as effectively as possible to achieve the larger purposes of the program.

m. There is an ability to recognize and use the informal authority of individual board members which arises not out of their specific assignments on the board but from their power, connections, wealth, age, or ability.

n. In case of internal conflict, the group has the capacity to examine the situation objectively, identify the sources of difficulty, and remedy them.

o. Most important of all, the board members share a clear understanding of and commitment to the cause which the agency serves.

Section I
HIGH STANDARDS

***ESSENCE: Christian leaders must set standards
for business ethics.***

JESUS SAID we are "salt and light" in this world. We represent Him. If the light is hidden, He asked, or the salt loses its flavor, what use is it? His point is clear: Both personally and organizationally, we must be transparent reflections of God's character.

God sets our standard of business practice for us; mediocrity or moral compromise are not true options.

A side benefit of high standards is that they give your board and senior executive an organization you can believe in.

Appropriate standards of excellence will be seen in these areas:

1. *Honesty*

Honesty is our only option as believers in Jesus Christ, who is "the way and the *truth* and the life." We are to tell the truth—to our employers, to our creditors, to our constituency, to our government, and to one another. Not partial truth, but the whole truth.

Let your conversation and life be thoroughly honest. Let your Yes be Yes and your No, No.

2. *Integrity*

Integrity in essence is doing what you say you will do and being who you profess to be. How good is your word? Can it be trusted? When you make agreements with staff, with financial institutions, with vendors—is it with confidence? Or do others fear you won't be able to keep your word?

A fine line divides faith and irresponsibility. To order

goods or services from a vendor *in the hope* that there will be money to pay for them is irresponsible. To develop a plan of projected income to provide for those goods and services is an act of faith.

Integrity requires paying your bills as agreed and on time. If you find yourself in a difficult situation due to unexpected misfortune or gross neglect, go to your creditors and inform them of your plight. Make a reasonable offer to pay what is owed, even if it now includes additional fees or interest. God honors an honest heart that pursues integrity.

3. *Confidentiality*

Never share unpublished information or psychological insight into a person, even if you were not asked to "keep this confidential." Relationships are built on trust. Trust is warranted when confidences are kept.

4. *Avoiding conflict of interest*

One reason our laws require a nonprofit corporation to be governed by a board of directors is to ensure that no one directly "profits" financially from a nonprofit business. A *group* of people govern the organization to protect it.

When an individual on a board of directors casts a vote that benefits himself personally (or his family or firm), he has a conflict of interest.

Frequently, board members happen to be in a business where they can give your organization a reasonable rate for service, and both the group and the board member benefit. In this situation we suggest the board be totally aware of costs and benefits involved, and that the member involved excuse himself from the room while the vote is being taken to avoid the appearance of an inappropriate conflict of interest. (See the sample policy memo on conflict of interest in the Appendix.)

Similarly, when a board member has personal interests—which are termed a *vested* interest—in some aspect of the organization's service, his judgment can be biased on a variety of issues before the board. For example, if a board member has a son employed in the organization, it will be difficult for him to vote to shut down the division where his son works. Guard yourself from difficult situations by abstaining from voting on issues that involve your vested interest.

Section J
LEGAL MATTERS

4

ESSENCE: **The legal "buck" stops at the board level.**

WHEN THE NEED for legal counsel arises, knowing exactly what the board wants before going to the attorney is ideal. When the board knows what it wants done and is in complete agreement, you can maximize the attorney's time...and your money!

Ask your attorney to explain the personal liability each board member assumes for organizational default. You will want to know how your family and your personal estate would be held responsible for any mismanagement on the part of the organization.

Boards often want to select an attorney as a board member—to save fees, as well as for his counsel. But we have seen it work just as well to have an attorney available to serve the board at any time, but who does not regularly sit in on board meetings.

These criteria can help you evaluate and select an attorney:

a. Does he have a positive or a negative orientation? Your attorney should value your organization's purpose and goals, and want to help you get there legally—rather than being focused on why you can't get there!

b. Does he have a grasp of a Christian approach to arbitration? What is his experience in this kind of process?

c. Can he express himself clearly in written and verbal form so staff and board can clearly understand issues and options?

d. What is his track record in court (or in keeping his clients out of court)? Although you, as a Christian organization, may not ever go to court against your brother, what do you do if you are sued by someone else? If you ever have to go to court, you'll want someone working for you whose track record there is strong.

Here are more thoughts on seeking legal counsel, as well as on the maintenance of legal documents:

1. *Before you seek legal counsel on a matter, ask...*

a. Is this primarily a moral or ethical issue, rather than a legal one? When Ronald Reagan was being interviewed while a presidential candidate, he was asked about the issue of homosexual rights. His comment: "There are many things which are legal that aren't morally right."
    Board members need to make such distinctions as well, and realize that even if an attorney advises that there is no legal hindrance to a certain proposed action, moral and ethical restraints may still require that the action not be taken.

b. Can we draft a needed legal document in our own words, saving the attorney's time and our money?

c. As a board, are we in complete agreement about what we actually want accomplished? Reaching this understanding is necessary before seeking legal counsel. On the other hand, don't simply sort out as a board what you together think is right and not check with an attorney if, in fact, one is needed.

2. *When you should ALWAYS check with an attorney:*

a. Before entering into any major or complex contractual agreement.

b. Before answering accusations from cults, dissidents, community trouble makers and others.

c. Before you respond to someone who is trying to sue you. In our present legal system, many "sue-them-for-all-they-are-worth" people are looking for reasons to seek litigation. If someone calls threatening to sue the organization or individual board members, check with your attorney immediately.

d. Before you enter public confrontations involving social issues with complicated legal aspects, such as abortion, pornography, and legalized gambling. Know your legal limits, as well as the legal land mines. You don't want to come off as the foolish-looking subject of unwanted media attention.

Don't try to be an attorney, but know how to deal with people who may be much more sophisticated in the legal field than you are. If you don't know your legal limits, your adversary could make you look silly, which in turn reflects poorly on the board and the organization you represent.

3. *Legal documents you are required to maintain:*

a. articles of incorporation
b. constitution and bylaws
c. board meeting minutes
d. tax exemption papers

Section K
MANAGING MONEY

**ESSENCE: *A board member's adequate survey
of the organization's finances takes less than
twenty minutes a month, unless there are problems
(while a bookkeeper may need
twenty or more hours).***

LIBRARIES ARE FULL of books on the subject of money management. In this section we'll look at just a few basic principles
of money management from a board perspective.

1. *Organizational balance—key to growth and health*

Earlier we talked about the balance that must be maintained between an organization's resources, operations,
service, and feedback. If this balance is not maintained,
negative consequences are predictable.

Suppose you have an organization with rapidly diminish-
ing resources, but a large dollar commitment to established
operations, services and feedback. Within a short period of
time, the operations will have to be cut back to the point at
which they can be funded with the resources. The same is
true of the service and, ultimately, the feedback as well.

Or, let's say you have a major resource base and considerable operations, but no ministry. Soon your donors will be
angry with the poor use of their money and they will stop
giving.

Or perhaps you have few resources, limited operations,
and a lot of service. You're on your way to bankruptcy.

You must maintain that delicate, productive balance.

2. *Budgeting*

A budget should be seen as a guideline, not a straitjack-
et. It's a target, not a whip. It is your guideline to see when
and where we are off our projections.

One way to keep budgeting in perspective is to review the following five-step process:

1. *generating money:* earning it, raising it, borrowing it

2. *bookkeeping and accounting:* handling funds in an accountable fashion

3. *budgeting:* controlling it, spending it, and controlling the spending

4K

4. *managing cash:* building reserves

5. *making money make money:* creatively using our capital base to increase our capital base

In the financial process, all five steps are important for an organization to be successful.

When starting an organization, it is particularly critical to focus on the first step because the process is sequential. You will have to focus more on generating dollars than you will on controlling dollars. The most brilliantly conceived budgeting and expense control system in the world is worthless if adequate dollars aren't being generated.

The board should direct the attention of the senior executive and executive staff toward generating dollars first, then focus on bookkeeping and controlling.

One of the things you will find from studying organizations is that the "get-by" organizations tend to focus on budgeting. The winning organizations—the ones that are growing rapidly and seem to be adequately funded—focus first on generating dollars. They don't stop at step three, but go on to budgeting and cash management. They are beginning to build reserves—as hedges against economic downturns, and so they don't have to borrow money to fund future projects.

The exceptional organizations are those that know how to generate dollars and how to manage cash properly, and then actually go on to have their money make money for them.

It's a constant temptation to boards to try to "get by" in the the organization's budgeting process and cash management. You may want to discuss the topic of money management at your next board retreat. The board's philosophy of money management will substantially affect what the organization will become in future decades.

3. Watching the trends—and more

In his book *Managing in Turbulent Times*, Peter Drucker writes: "Don't watch only the trends, but watch the changes in the trends." As a board member, you want to concentrate on identifying a few vital signs within the organization, the five to seven financial variables that are most indicative of the health of your organization. Mark these variables on charts showing five- to ten-year trends, and begin to monitor which way the organization is moving.

The variables tracked by these charts can include:

- income and expense trends
- projected net income vs. actual net income
- payables
- receivables
- debts (short-term to long-term)
- net worth

To visually oriented people (and most of us are), one chart is worth ten thousand numbers. A few board members are much more numbers-oriented and will want to see the actual figures in detail, but most members just want to see a clear overview, and will ask for details if there is a concern or problem.

You may also want to establish some ratios and indexes. A ratio is a comparison of two variables with each other, while an index is a comparison of three or more key variables. Observing these ratios and indexes over time can save hours of anxiety. You will begin to see the trend lines of what is actually happening in your organization.

Ask yourself what three to seven key variables you want to watch. Chart them, as well as perhaps putting them into ratios or indexes. Chart them regardless of whether the person who is responsible for the numbers does it for you or not. Go out of your way to establish the context you need to watch the trends.

Note: When you are showing trends for accounts payable, show the trend line on cumulative accounts payable rather than monthly accounts payable, so you see the extent of your accumulated liability. Do the same with accounts receivable as well.

4. *Cash flow projections*

Cash flow projections are where most boards panic when they should relax—and relax when they should panic.

In most organizations, you can chart projected cash flow if your key financial variables remain somewhat consistent. You can predict high-income months and high-expense months. With these projections you can make more discerning financial decisions. For example, you would be able to avoid major new investments during a month in which, historically, income has been low and expense high.

5. *Financial reports*

"What do I have to know to do what I have to do?" This is the question that efficiency expert Si Simonson suggests we ask in deciding what management reports we need to see.

When you receive financial reports, they should always be accompanied by notes. Ask the bookkeeper or accountant to give you not only the numbers, but also his interpretation of what the numbers really mean.

Make sure you are getting accurate financial reports. You want to know if the reports are ball-park estimates, or if they show what has actually happened. All too often financial reports are "guesstimates" presented as realities.

Financial reports should be clear and comprehensive overviews of what is happening with the money. The most frequent problem with financial reports is that their numbers convey little meaning to most people. The typical board is given lots of financial data that is difficult to interpret because there is no context. Remember the principle: Nothing is meaningful without a context or comparison.

Let's say you are handed a financial report that indicates your organization is $50,000 in the red this month. Do you panic or breath a sigh of relief? Ask, "$50,000 compared to what?" If your projection was a $100,000 debt, you are in great shape. If it was $50,000 in the red, you are right on target. If your projection was $50,000 in the black, you are in deep trouble. Unless you know what was projected, you don't know how to properly interpret the actual results.

This is where visual charts come in handy. If you can visualize your cash situation in the context of cash flow projections, you can quickly determine negative and positive trends. Chart the projected information with a dotted line and the actual amounts with a solid line. Each month, add one short line to the chart and you have a totally new financial report comparing exactly where you are with where you are supposed to be. You can always be up to date once your basic charts are drawn.

If you are not getting the following key reports from your organization's accountant or financial office, you will want to request them:

- *monthly / annual budget*
- *cash flow projection*—to show seasonality
- *monthly or quarterly financial statement*—a moving picture of the flow of your money through the system
- *balance sheet*—a snapshot of your total value and net worth
- *annual report*—a summary of this year compared to previous years

6. *Bankruptcy*

Here are a few steps to help your organization avoid bankruptcy, or to help you work yourself out of a financial hole:

To avoid bankruptcy:

a. Have financial cushions.

b. Have safe debt/equity-ratio limits.

c. Have cash before you act, whenever possible.

d. Risk your own dollars, not lender dollars.

To work your way out of a hole:

a. Talk with your creditors and come up with a plan. Even though it may only be a relatively few dollars a month, you can work your way out.

b. Cut your expenses drastically and as rapidly as possible, including the hard decisions of releasing key people.

c. Focus on a plan to raise money.

d. Temporarily boost the percentage of your fund-raising budget.

Bankruptcy bears a tremendous price, beyond the moral and credibility issues. Perhaps greatest is the human price—mentally and emotionally—on those going through it.

Warning: If you're growing faster than your ability to repay development expenditures, you are growing too rapidly. Slow your growth and get within safer limits.

7. *Principles for managing money*

a. *Feed the goose.* Let the "organizational goose" grow, or you'll never have healthy eggs. At one point in the history of World Vision, the organization spent money on a computer to service its operational needs while children were actually starving in Korea. Some would say we should have spent all of our money on ministry. But if that had been the case, World Vision would probably be out of business today instead of generating hundreds of millions of dollars for needs around the world. Feed the organizational goose or it will never lay healthy eggs.

b. *Focus on the elephant first.* An Italian economist gave this profound advice: "If you are Noah and the ark is about to sink from too much weight, throw the elephants overboard first."

If you are looking at the financial condition of your organization, don't try to improve on the small line items. Focus on those items that generate major dollars, and eliminate the major expenditures. If you save only one percent on something that costs $1,000,000 a year, you save more than if you cut back ninety percent on something costing $10,000 a year.

c. *Build three-legged stability into your cash flow.* Any organization that depends primarily on only one source of revenue is particularly vulnerable to losing its financial base. As quickly as it is financially feasible, begin developing two additional income sources for your organization so you have at least three income sources. This may not be practical for a church where all or almost all of its income is from donations in the offering plate. But for other organizations and corporations, a "three-legged stool" is a viable financial model.

To give a tangible example: At Masterplanning Group, income is generated from three main sources—consulting, resources, and seminars. If any one of them were cut off unexpectedly, the firm wouldn't be nearly as vulnerable as it would be if it originally had only one or two sources of income.

d. *Avoid fixed expenses when possible.* Fixed expenses on a variable income can quickly get you into trouble. As the saying goes, "When your outgo exceeds your income, your upkeep will be your downfall."

e. *Look for "cash cows."* A cash cow is a product or program that keeps generating dollars year after year. You buy a cow once but you can milk it for several years, and it keeps bringing in income as long as you have it. Look for those products or services that will generate an ongoing financial base for your organization.

f. *Be aware that start-up programs are not as financially predictable as existing programs.* Whenever you start a new program it is extremely difficult to predict accurately what your income, expenses, or cash flow needs will be. For example, when we first started the Love Loaf program at World Vision, we tried to predict the amount, source. and timing of income. We found it impossible. But now, having been established for several years, the program has become a fairly predictable income source. It's an example of a "cash cow" that continues generating a substantial number of dollars year after year.

g. *Guard the motive of your heart in handling money matters.* You are one of the stewards of the funds God provides your organization. Be faithful in serving Him with the funds He entrusts to you. As a faithful servant be diligent (work hard), prudent (careful, somewhat conservative), and courageous (willing to risk when necessary, and willing to say no when needed).

KEEP GROWING in your ability to manage money wisely!

Section L
MASTER PLANNING

ESSENCE: *A Master Plan is a written statement of a group's assumptions about its direction, organization, and resources.*

A BOARD MEMBER'S responsibility is to review, refine, approve and track the Master Plan drafted by the senior executive with help from the executive staff. Once a Master Plan is in place, you become a servant helping the executive team reach your organizational goals. Without a Master Plan in place, the negative consequences are predictable.

Your current Master Plan is a context for all future decision making—no plan...no context! Having no Master Plan and trying to build team harmony is like trying to conduct an orchestra where each musician is playing a different composition. The Master Plan becomes the same piece of music for your organization.

If your senior executive is an entrepreneurial leader, it may be especially difficult to keep a clear understanding of the direction he is heading. To the extent you commit your Master Plan to writing, the board and staff can begin working together with combined strength to accomplish your dreams.

When designing and developing a Master Plan, you will find several advantages to seeking outside counsel:

1. *You acquire the objectivity of an outsider who can help you work together.* With board members coming from a variety of professional backgrounds (business, industry, education, military), it is quite possible—in fact, probable—that they would suggest very different planning processes, perhaps even diametrically opposite processes. Agreement in such a group is typically difficult. Having an outside consultant helps your group come together in planning. He will lead your group to a three-way level of unity—board, senior executive, and executive staff. He will help your entire team come to a unified understanding of the plan, the goals, the

organizational structure, the budgeting process, and the tracking system for your organization's Master Plan.

2. *You gain the experience of a expert who has gone through the planning process many times.* The planning process may seem like a swampy, snake-infested jungle to you, but to him it's a sure-footed, familiar path. He has proven himself many times with organizations like yours.

3. *You become accountable to a knowledgeable outsider who can come back to you regularly and ask, "How are you coming on your plan?"*

4L

In the experience of Masterplanning Group International (with more than a hundred clients), it is best to have the senior executive do the first draft of each step in the Master Plan process. Typically, he is best able to provide a broad context for the rest of the group to do their planning—for two reasons. First, he is the directional leader and has a feel for where the organization should be headed. Second, he usually has the broadest and deepest experience in the organization as a whole. These factors are critical, even though he may not be as technically adept as one of the other executive staff, or as experienced in business as one of the board members.

When we use the term "directional leader" in describing the senior executive, we do not mean to imply someone who is dictatorial. There is a distinct difference between the two, as seen in this nutshell description of the three organizational leadership styles:

1. *Dictator:* The dictatorial leader says, "This is the way it is going to be," and others follow accordingly, without question.

2. *Director:* The directional leader points the way for the group's action, always utilizing the skill and expertise of the executive staff; the board reviews, refines and approves. (In the case of putting together the Master Plan, the directional leader does the first

draft, involving the staff at appropriate points, then presenting it for the board's refinement and approval.)

3. *Committee:* A group provides the true leadership for the organization, in which case the senior executive is more of a maintainer.

THE PROCESS

Masterplanning Group uses the acrostic D.O.C.T.O.R. to identify the actual Master Plan process—partly because it helps in memorizing the outline for the process, and partly because of the health symbolism. If you have a pain in your arm, and you go to a doctor whose own arm hurts, and who has never had a patient who did NOT have a hurt arm, he will say you are normal. The only way a doctor can tell you what is really wrong with you is if he knows the look of a normal, healthy body. The reason most leaders do not know what is wrong with their organization is that they have never seen a healthy organization, and particularly one that follows a complete and working Master Plan.

Details of the D.O.C.T.O.R. planning process take up an entire notebook, and the process typically requires months of work to implement. We can't hope to cover the process adequately in a few pages, but the overview below will give you a feel for the direction and the various components that need to be in a Master Plan.

"D"—Direction

The profound directional question is,

What do we do next and why?

Whatever planning process you use, it needs to start with a clear definition of the *needs* you feel deeply burdened by and uniquely qualified to meet. This should be followed closely by a statement of *purpose* (why you exist), and then a statement of *objectives* (the activities in which you will continue to be involved). These three areas—needs, purpose, and objectives—are what we refer to as *focus*.

In determining objectives for each category of activity in your organization, you should answer these eight questions:

a. What major milestones have we already accomplished?

b. What ideas have we had that we should consider turning into goals for the future?

c. What three obstacles are keeping us from reaching our full potential?

d. What are our three greatest resources?

e. What are our top three specific, measurable targets of accomplishment (goals) for the next ninety days?

f. What are our top three specific, measurable targets of accomplishment for the next two years?

g. What are our top three possible targets of accomplishment for the next two to five years?

h. What are the top three goals we are dreaming of accomplishing five to twenty years from now?

"O"—*Organization*

You do not know who you need on your staff until you have a clear understanding of what you want to do. Once you know what you are going to do—which is accomplished in the directional step—you can move to organization.

The essential questions to ask in the organization step

are these:

Who is responsible for what?

Who is responsible for whom?

Do we have the right people in the right places?

The three primary tools Masterplanning Group uses for setting up the organizational structure are these:

- an organizational chart
- a position focus sheet for each position (see the sample in the Appendix)
- a role preference inventory for each person

One word of caution: The most difficult step of the planning process to work through without outside objectivity in the organizational step. The subjective assumptions you are making about who should hold what position within the organization makes it difficult for you to reorganize the staff.

Once you know what you are going to do (direction), and who is going to do it (organization), you are ready for step three.

"C"—*Cash*

The vital questions in a cash management are:

What are our projected income, expenses, and net?

Can we afford it? or *How can we afford it?*

In this step of the planning process you establish your budget, cash flow projections, and financial trend charts.

When you have these three dimensions—direction, organization, and cash—spelled out in writing and your group can agree on them with a three-level agreement (the board, the senior executive and the executive staff), you have a Master Plan.

Of course, your own approach to determining these three dimensions does not have to match the process taught by Masterplanning Group International. You can use any system you like.

Once your entire team is "playing off the same sheet of music" in these three areas, you'll have made significant progress. However—at this point most groups tend to lose focus, and the Master Plan becomes a notebook on a shelf. What is typically missing are the last three steps of the D.O.C.T.O.R. process.

4L

"T"—*Tracking*

In the tracking step there is really only one important question:

Are we on target?

Of course, tracking assumes you have goals in place. Your tracking questions are the reporting process.

Masterplanning Group recommends one reporting procedure for everyone—from board member to first-year staff volunteer. There are six simple yet highly revealing questions to ask. For a detailed explanation of this simplified reporting procedure, see Section T in this chapter.

Tracking is the step which reports your quantity of results. However, it does not guarantee the quality of those results. For that, you move to the Overall Evaluation step.

"O"—*Overall Evaluation*

In overall evaluation you ask this question:

*Are we achieving the quality we expect
and demand of ourselves?*

Once you have your evaluation questionnaires (see the sample form in the Appendix) for the staff, for the programs and for the overall organization, you have your quality assurance program.

Based on what you find in the Overall Evaluation step, you can make appropriate refinements.

"R"—*Refinement*

The primary refinement question is this:

*How can we be more effective and efficient
as an organization?*

In the refinement step, develop process charts to help you quickly identify exactly needed changes for achieving the efficiency and effectiveness you want.

When the senior executive has completed the first draft for each of these steps, the board can review in ten minutes what may have taken ten hours of creative discussion time to create.

Once you have all six D.O.C.T.O.R steps in place, you have a Master Plan that will continue to function as you refine it year after year.

Section M
THE OVERVIEW:
KEEPING THE BIG PICTURE

*ESSENCE: **Nothing is meaningful
without a context.***

4M

YOUR PRIMARY SOURCE of overview is your master plan. Your primary source of objectivity is outside counsel. Once you have a master plan you can keep a constant overview of your direction, organization, and money, and with occasional outside input you can retain objectivity.

One of the key roles the board plays for the senior executive and executive staff is keeping a consistent overview. The staff is too involved in executing their given part of the program to perform this function.

The more committed a person is to the group, the less objective they become. Therefore, by the time you get to be the senior executive of an organization or on the board, you are far less objective about the organization than you were as a new member. That is why outside counsel or outside perspective is often so valuable.

Four primary points can help you regain an overview of an organization.

1. *Prayer* gives you an eternal perspective on the organizational needs.

2. *The directional statement* gives you an overview of the short-, mid- and long-range goals within an organization. It lets you view all the goals of the organization, not just those of a certain department or division.

3. *The organizational chart* gives you an overview of the people. By reviewing your organizational chart you can look at a decision in terms of its impact on all staff.

4. *The financial charts* give you an overview of the finances.

In your personal life you'll want to keep a slightly different overview. As you are making any major personal decision, you will want to observe how your decision affects seven basic areas of life (listed alphabetically):

1. family and marriage
2. financial
3. personal growth
4. physical
5. professional
6. social
7. spiritual

Remember that an overview can still be subjective, internalized, and in-grown in its perspective. Looking at something objectively means that you are looking at it from an outside person's perspective without the traditional assumptions that may limit your thinking.

Three sources can help you become objective about an organization:

1. *Outside counsel.* Proctor & Gamble commits approximately thirteen percent of its income to outside advertising agencies when a good percentage of that could be retained by an inside agency. They insist on maintaining an outside agency for one reason—objectivity!

Outside counsel does not have to be paid, professional counsel, although that is certainly one source of objectivity. Another can be friends and colleagues who work in a parallel organization but in a different geographic area. Inviting an outside friend to review your organization and show you things you are not currently seeing could also be very helpful.

2. *Data.* No matter how excited you feel about what is going on, if you are consistently losing "X" thousands of

dollars per month, the data will sooner or later tend to objectify your thinking.

3. *Standard checklists.* Checklists such as a list of thirty questions to ask before any major decision, or the list of brainstorming questions in the Appendix, help bring an objective perspective that isn't available if you're just sitting in a room thinking by yourself. If you have a list someone else has created, it forces you to ask new questions.

Section N
PLANNING HOMEWORK
INTO YOUR SCHEDULE

ESSENCE: *Being on a board and not doing your homework is like winking at someone in the dark.*

ALWAYS DO YOUR HOMEWORK before a board meeting! On a board you need to initiate as well as respond. You need to think ahead, not just try to keep up—and the key is doing your homework.

When you've prepared your homework, you have three distinct advantages:

1. You have a wiser, more informed perspective about the issues being considered—you're less likely to be fooled.

2. You know where you want to go.

3. People respect your comments.

Our friend Dr. Bob Andringa has a basic philosophy of influencing organizations: "If you want to influence the way a committee is headed, simply volunteer to take the responsibility. You will be able to influence a high percentage of the committee's decisions."

Homework is not only the key to influencing boards, it is a key to having effective meetings. If everyone does his homework, the meeting goes smoothly. If members do not do their homework everything bogs down. There are three areas to consider on the subject of homework:

1. *Use a pre-board meeting checklist.*

   a. Mark your calendar well in advance of the board meeting to do your homework.

   b. Keep your own financial graphics even if the board doesn't. If they do not keep overview charts of the data you receive, do your own charts or offer to help them design the overview for the charts they will then maintain.

   c. Review the agenda carefully! See which items need your pre-meeting thoughts, and which ones you would like to influence specifically. Think independently about the agenda. Sort out your ideas and convictions so you know exactly how you look at each item on the agenda. Be able to identify shallow thinking quickly and be ready to suggest alternative solutions to the problems presented.

2. *Research.*

Most good research questions are essentially the same as Rudyard Kipling's basic questions: Who? What? Why? Where? When? How?...and How Much? These are excellent research questions by which to think through any item on the agenda.

Another researching technique is the speed modeling trip. Visit the leadership at a church or organization similar to your own (though preferably somewhat larger or more experienced in doing what your organization does). Ask questions that bring to light their successful or unsuccessful experiences. Once you have been on a speed modeling trip, the people you've met will be contacts you can call for help in the future—"We're going to vote on a complicated issue next Wednesday night, and I thought I'd call and explain it to you and just ask if you've had any experience on it . . ." You can gain new perspectives as your contact tells you what did or didn't work for his church or organization in a similar situation. By the time you get to the board meeting, you have a broader view of the issue.

4N

Doing research often pays substantial dividends by increasing your ability to influence the other board members to see the rightness of moving in the direction you suggested. Or, it may help you see that the others are right. Doing research can save you the embarrassment of suggesting something that would only prove to be unwise.

3. *Prepare to initiate as well as respond.*

Consider these questions to help you be an initiator:

a. What do I want to praise or appreciate?

b. Is there something in the group which may be explosive?

c. What are the next three steps I would take, if I were the senior executive?

d. What can I prepare as a report from my subcommittee?

e. On which upcoming decisions should I do independent research?

f. Who should I talk to about an upcoming issue before the meeting?

g. You may want to ask the senior executive or the chairman how you can help by doing research for the upcoming meeting.

Do "above and beyond" research on key issues to be discussed. You will rarely be sorry you have done extra research on a discreet basis prior to a board meeting. On the other hand, when a discussion goes the wrong way and you haven't thought through your own position, you may find yourself wishing you had done more independent thinking.

Research takes time. That is why we suggest that, if you are serving on a board, your should avoid taking on additional major responsibilities. If done correctly, board service takes a considerable amount of time.

Section O
POLICY SETTING

**ESSENCE: *Policy tells what we always do,
and what we never do.***

IF YOU ASK the average person to describe the role of any
board, one of the responses you're likely to hear is "estab-
lishing policy." Yet the same person may be unable to define
the word *policy*.

Policy is what we always do, and what we never do. This
simple definition makes it easy for you to begin drafting
simple policies. As you get these policies set, the staff can
then make automatic decisions without having to check with
the board.

Here are guidelines to help you write organizational
policies:

1. K.I.S.S.—"Keep It Simple, Servant." As you agree to
serve the group by drafting policy, keep it as simple as
possible.

2. Include your reasons for setting any given policy.
Present not only the rule, but the rationale.

3. Some people enjoy writing policy more than others.
If someone on your board particularly enjoys doing the first
draft of a policy, and you find that he does it exceptionally
well...let him.

(For a policy statement format others have found useful,
see the sample policy statement in the Appendix.)

Section P
PRAYING

*ESSENCE: **Keep asking yourself, "Are we acting as though God is dead—or alive?"***

EVEN THE MOST devout believers forget sometimes that God is actually alive. As you keep reminding yourself of that, and balance your facts and faith, you provide an inspiring model of leadership for the entire group.

Being a Christian leader provides a dynamic tension between prayer and action. Both are realistic responsibilities and must be treated with care. You cannot simply pray for the needs of the people; you must act on them. At the same time, you can't simply act on the needs of the people; you must pray for them. (Board members of churches find specific scriptural direction to pray for the sick—both the physically sick and sick of heart—in James 5:14-15.) This tension between prayer and action is always present in any organization with Christian leadership.

1. *How to pray*

You may say, "Of course I know how to pray, but I simply don't feel comfortable praying in public." Yet people expect, or at least hope, that as a board member you will feel comfortable praying for them "on the spot"—now! (If you feel uncomfortable praying in public, we recommend the book *Praying: How to Start and Keep Going* [Regal, 1981], which Bobb has written with a senior pastor, Dr. James W. Hagelganz. This book is particularly valuable in helping you feel comfortable praying with people who are hurting.)

2. *Praying*

There are many reasons a Christian leader needs to pray. Among them are the following:

a. It does move the hand of God, as God heals people and moves in the affairs of men.

b. It restores our eternal perspective of the problem, and reminds us that God is real.

c. It corrects our attitudes. The simple act of dropping to our knees corrects our pride, our self-centeredness, and our self-dependency.

4P

d. It gives others hope and encouragement as they hear us praying on their behalf.

e. It restores our own faith, and builds the faith of others.

3. *Praying before meetings*

There are tremendous advantages in having prayer before your board meetings:

a. It gets all of the members' hearts ready for the spiritual side of the business.

b. It relieves much tension from the individual members who may have had difficult days at home or work.

c. It strengthens the relationships between board members, as each member prays for the burdens of the other members. (At the next board meeting, check to see what the answers have been.)

Every organizational unit is a direct reflection of the leadership that has been given, for good or for bad. If you expect your entire group to be a praying group, it is important that you model a life of prayer before them.

Section Q
PROBLEM SOLVING

ESSENCE: *Moses (in Exodus 18) learned to deal only with problems that no one else at a lower level could solve; the same should be true of boards.*

ASK THE SENIOR EXECUTIVE and staff to solve all possible problems. Where appropriate, assign board-level problems to a committee to solve. Avoid taking the time of the whole board. The whole board should deal only with the truly tough issues. Once the board is only dealing with the major problems, it can devote itself to deep analysis and critical problem solving—and still adjourn on time.

Solving one problem, however, often leads only to another problem. You rarely get to the point on a board where you have no pressing problems needing to be solved. If you do, you may not be growing fast enough. As you feel the press of numerous problems, remember Richard Sloma's statement in his book *No-Nonsense Management:* "Never try to solve all the problems all at once; make them line up one by one."

1. *How to help staff solve their own problems*

One key to helping staff solve their own problems is to give them clear policies .

Another is to keep a list of resource people and organizations who specialize in solving particular problems. Staff can refer to the list and find the help they need.

Give the senior executive progressive freedom to decide issues at the staff level. It is also useful to spot natural problem solvers on the staff or board and use them as "in-house consultants."

2. *Nine-step process for solving board-sized problems*

The following nine questions can help you deal with any

problem that forces its way up the organizational chart to the board:

a. Specifically what is the problem?

b. What is the context (framework, background, or process) of the problem?

c. What was the central cause of the problem? What principle has been violated?

4Q

d. What are our top three options as solutions?

e. What is our best option?

f. Will this option actually remove the cause, or just remove the symptoms? (What does it take to really *win?*)

g. What is the value/price balance with this option?

h. What is right (morally, ethically, legally)?

i. If someone else could solve this problem eighty percent as well as we could—who would that be? (Delegate!)

3. *Common problems faced by boards—and possible first steps toward solution*

Some problems seem to come before many boards consistently. Here are some of them, and how we would deal with them:

a. *Outgrowing the organization's facility*

First, appoint a three- or four-person study committee to verify the need and to recommend quick, creative, alternative solutions. Second, ask all board members to use their network to identify a church facility consultant with a proven track record. Third, ask the committee to report to the whole board in a specified number of months.

b. *A moral problem within the staff*

First, the senior executive and two or three board members are assigned as a special support group to the person. Second, review all appropriate Scriptures as a group. Third, approach the person (or persons) with an intent of restoration according to scriptural principles. Fourth, make a follow-up report to the board, if the board is aware of the situation.

c. *A sudden drop in income to red-line level*

First, check the accuracy of the report (sometimes an incomplete or faulty interpretation of data makes the situation look tragic when it really is not). Second, do not just start talking about how much you need money. Start talking about needs you see in the con-stituency your organization is serving—in other words, restoring the dream. Third, drastically reduce spending by the staff until financial balance is regained. Fourth, appoint two or three people (as creative a group as possible) to create break-through ideas to generate new funds.

d. *The senior executive's sudden resignation, without notice*

First, the chairman of the board needs to be debriefed by the senior executive concerning his views of the master plan and various families on the staff and within the organization. Second, create a "leaving" checklist. Third, review the master plan to see what has changed. Fourth, start the executive search process. (See the recruiting process outlined in the Appendix.)

e. *Apathy or sagging morale in the group*

First, encourage the senior executive. Second, start looking at the target group's needs rather than the needs within the organization. Third, set three crystal-clear, ninety-day goals for each staff person. Fourth, visit and interview some group members to ask what is wrong...and listen carefully. Fifth, insist on positive staff attitudes.

4Q

f. *Lack of trained leaders*

First, make sure your organizational chart is clear and up-to-date. Second, ask a sub-committee to develop a top-to-bottom leadership development process for your organization. Third, commit a certain percentage of budget to support the above program.

g. *Lack of clear vision*

First, appoint a standing committee on the planning process. Second, focus your attention on the needs of your target group. Let your heart be broken by their needs. Third, dream of ways to meet their needs. Fourth, put your ideas into a Master Plan.

h. *A church split*

First, pray together if possible. Second, spell out your organizational assumptions remembering that "all miscommunication is a result of differing assumptions." Find where you are disagreeing fundamentally enough to cause a split. Third, call in outside counsel to clarify, negotiate, arbitrate or explain and discuss the differences, leading toward cooperation instead of conflict.

i. *A tumble in morale right after a move into a costly new facility*

First, focus your group on needs outside the group. Second, set a new stretching, but realistic ninety-day goal (specific and measurable) that is service oriented. Third, begin encouraging, appreciating and recognizing everyone. Keep being as positive as possible about the future!

j. *A key board member has joined the staff fulltime— should he resign?*

Yes, he should resign from his board position.

k. *Explosive growth* (a good problem!)

First, concentrate on a Master Plan. Second, concentrate on developing leaders to be able to absorb the new people. Third, concentrate on facility expansion. People do not tend to continue coming to an overcrowded facility. (A rule of thumb by church facilities consultant Joe Kimbel: "When a facility is eighty-percent full, growth will begin to level off.")

Problem solving requires endless hours of discussion, probing, analysis, synthesis—all the problem-solving processes. On the other hand, when your board makes a decision that solves a problem, you'll experience a great deal of personal and group satisfaction.

Section R
PROTOCOL

*ESSENCE: Protocol is doing what is right...
at the right time...in the right way.*

TRAIN YOURSELF to work through the anxiety of walking into someone else's personal crisis, or other awkward situations. Feeling anxiety in certain situations is common to everyone. When you finally break through, you can consistently provide leadership in protocol for the entire board, in situations such as these:

4R

1. *A personal crisis in a staff or board member's life*

Whenever a major personal crisis happens in another's life, there is a predictable, uncomfortable feeling that comes with wanting to approach a person appropriately, to be supportive in a difficult situation. Some examples: when a person is relieved from staff; there is death in the family; death of a fellow member of the board; emotionally difficult period following retirement; major sickness or accident; difficult resignations; divorce.

Realizing there's nothing wrong with feeling uncomfortable will help you work your way through this anxiety. Specialize in doing the right things that other board members may feel uncomfortable doing.

One of your most rewarding roles on the board may be helping someone go through a personal crisis. With a sensitive and caring response, the following appropriate actions can be very helpful:

a. Express your personal support and love regardless of any professional frustrations with the person. Separate the person from the position. You can fire a person who has failed in his work and still love the person.

b. Offer to serve during this crisis time. Try to find

something you can do personally to help the person or the family.

c. Offer to pray for them. Not, "I will be praying for you," but rather, "May I pray for you right now?"

d. Send a personal, supportive note if appropriate. We know of one elder statesman, Carlton Booth, the secretary of World Vision's board, who has sent probably thousands of notes of personal encouragement to people in hard times.

e. Remember that it is better to feel awkward and do something, than to feel guilty for not having done anything.

2. *When a new executive staff person's family arrives.*

a. Write a warm, supportive letter of welcome prior to their arrival in your city.

b. Invite them to lunch, dinner or breakfast in their first month of arrival.

c. Call during the first week and offer to help in any way, i.e., helping children find schools, helping them find various services like laundries, grocery stores, drug stores. Tell them you are happy to have them here. Say it with enthusiasm and meaning.

d. The first time you visit their home, take some small gift (can be homemade) for house warming.

e. For the first month, don't expect them to know your name or be able to remember anyone's name. Repeat your name when you meet to keep from embarrassing them and to help reinforce their memory, until it's obvious they remember your name.

f. As you sense the time is right, offer to introduce the new staff person to key contacts in the area, such as service clubs, banks, attorneys. Make your local network available to them.

g. Go out of your way to ensure the comfort of the spouse and children in their adjustment to a new city.

h. Think up creative ways you can add to this list over a lifetime.

4R

3. *Candidates for staff visit your organization.*

a. Offer to take them for a meal (you always pay!).

b. Offer to answer questions they may have.

c. Offer a tour of the area.

d. Write a supportive, personal note after their visit ...even if they were not selected.

e. Select the two or three positive things you see in them as a person or as a professional and complement them even if you don't feel they may be right for the position.

You may assume that this is the responsibility of the senior executive. In many ways it is. You may want to check with the current senior executive and see if he is comfortable with you playing this gracious role. It would be meaningful to the new person to be welcomed by board members as well as by the senior executive.

4. *Funeral for senior executive or staff*

a. Participate financially in flowers sent from the board, but sending flowers from your family, if you were especially close, would of course also be appropriate.

b. Express your attitude of personal love and support. See if there is anything you can do to serve.

c. Write a personal letter to the survivors expressing what the person meant to you, including separate letters to each child as well as spouse.

d. Mark your calendar one week, one month and one year in the future to call the family to see if there is anything you can do to help. Call even if they have moved to a different city.

e. Offer to pray. Again, don't just say you'll pray, but offer to pray together with them while you're there.

5. *Retirement of senior executive or executive staff*

The board as a whole should do the following:

a. Host a dinner to honor the person. Never do a roast. It is negative and more harmful psychologically to the person than it is helpful...especially at retirement. They have years to wonder "Did that person really mean the negative comment or were they just kidding?" Scripture warns, whatever is good and positive, think on these things, not the negative things. You may want to invite friends from the community to the dinner as well as members from your group.

b. Give an appropriate plaque which all of the board members have signed.

c. Give a love gift (one to three days salary per year of service; for example, three years times $100 a day equals a $300 gift; for a much-loved senior executive, twenty years times $100 per day times three days equals $6,000). A parting retirement gift is not a place to be cheap. This person has given a good share of their life to help you and your organization achieve what you have. You need to say thank you in a meaningful way.

d. Give the spouse a tangible gift as well, the cost of the spouse's gift depends somewhat on the amount of service they have given the organization.

e. Discuss retirement benefits openly with the retiring person.

f. Have a board prayer of departing blessing.

g. Encourage the group to write personal appreciation letters shortly after the person retires.

6. *Retirement of senior executive or executive staff*

These are responses individual board members should take:

a. Write a letter of appreciation remembering the good times and the contribution that person has made to your personal life.

b. Mark your calendar to call two or three times in the months ahead to express continued personal care and to see how the transitional adjustment is coming. (It is often extremely difficult!) The retiree may have many self-doubts, questioning his contribution to the organization, and the friendship of staff and board. Your phone calls assure him of his contribution and of your continuing relationship with him even though the professional relationship has changed.

c. To talk with the retired leader about problems that are developing with the new leader is extremely inappropriate, since these problems are not the retired leader's responsibility. So don't burden the retired leader with something for which he has no authority to make changes. Typically retired executives feel frustrated, guilty, and angry if they realize problems are developing about which they can do nothing.

7. *Extended sickness or accident involving the senior executive or executive staff.*

Anyone on extended sick leave almost always feel forgotten. Show compassion by staying in touch.

The board as a whole should:

a. Send flowers or an appropriate gift immediately.

b. With sensitivity, explain insurance and group benefits (or the lack of them) so the family knows what to count on.

Individual board members should:

a. Mark your calendar to call or write notes and check with the family or person periodically as appropriate.

b. Be especially supportive during this time. Families are fragile, budgets are tight and personal confidence typically at an all-time low. Be extremely sensitive as you relate to a family in sickness or accident.

c. As you visit him, don't talk to any length about board issues or the organization's problems. It can easily overtax a recovering person. In ten minutes you can share enough to overwhelm a sick person for a month of inactive reflection. Sending flowers is optional. Cards are always welcome.

8. *Senior executive or executive staff is relieved (fired)*

The board as a whole should—as appropriate, and on a modified basis—treat this situation as though it were a retirement.

Individual board members should do the following:

a. Express your personal support, care, and love.

b. Offer to help locate other work if you have appropriate contacts. Caution: never promise what you can't deliver.

c. Write a letter focusing on the contribution that was made (even though it was inadequate to keep the position), and express your regrets that it didn't work out.

Even for someone in an executive position who is eventually regarded as a negative roadblock to the progress of the organization, a look back will usually bring to mind one or more major contributions he made in his tenure, while putting in consistent hours and demonstrating a willing commitment to serve the organization. All this is sufficient reason to honor him.

But not honoring the man after his many years of experience sends a loud and clear message to the other staff and board members that "service here is not appreciated." The current staff thinks: "I'm going to work here for years, spend hundreds of hours on behalf of this organization —when I could have been making real money or building my own business—only to be dumped in the end, and not even get a letter of appreciation!"

It's easy to see the incredible value of recognizing contribution even for someone who has been fired for lack of performance.

9. *Addition of new members*

(This section applies especially to local church boards.)

a. If new members are added to the board, it is important that each member of the board communicate a welcome to the new member outside the group board meeting by telephoning, offering to take them to a meal or sending a letter of congratulations on their appointment to the board. Offer to help make the adjustment to the board as easy as possible.

b. For new members who have joined the church, board members should communicate welcome whenever possible, as above. As you get to know the new members, try to introduce them around to people you think they would enjoy.

    Pastor Larry DeWitt of Calvary Community Church in Thousand Oaks, California, has a strategy he calls "tying strings." He gets together two members together who have a lot in common. As a result, they come to church partly to meet each other and are less dependent on the pastors to meet all their needs. This would be an ideal role for a board member to play, especially in a local church.

10. *Retiring board members*

The board as a whole should do the following:

a. Give the retiring member a plaque showing the number of years of service and, ideally, signed by all the fellow members.

b. Show public appreciation—in the organization's newsletter, for example, or at a public dinner.

c. Possibly schedule a special event for a retiring member—for example, a dinner with spouses. If you feel a dinner is too costly, host a special party at the member's last meeting.

d. Always focus on the contribution the retiring member has made to the group and what he or she has contributed to your life personally.

e. Send a letter of appreciation and recognition from the chairman or senior executive for the retiring member's contribution.

f. In your last meeting together, join in prayer together, praying specifically for the retiring member.

Besides the board's collective response, other board members should personally convey their appreciation for a retiring member's unique contribution to their lives. This should be done apart from the board meeting environment—via a telephone call, letter, or over lunch.

11. *Ambassadors of the board*

Occasionally you will have the responsibility of representing the entire board as its ambassador of good will. You will participate in speed modeling trips to other organizations. You will attend conventions and conferences on the board's behalf. You will represent the board at community events or possibly even media interviews.

Your board should fund its ambassadors properly, or stand ready to reimburse within mutually agreed upon limits. They need to represent you properly—or they shouldn't be sent.

If you are chosen to represent the group, keep in mind these guidelines:

a. If you don't know what the appropriate dress is for the occasion, then overdress. You can always take off your tie. You don't want to represent your organization in short sleeves if it turns out everyone else is dressed in a suit. It is perfectly acceptable to ask your host and hostess ahead of time what the appropriate dress code is. But remember, you are representing the entire board, not just yourself, and you don't want to be underdressed for the occasion.

b. Focus on being...

- *gracious* — smiling, warm, supportive, not cold, aloof.

- *serving*—give as well as receive; even though you are guest, focus on giving a small gift, a service, a smile, a word of encouragement.

- *generous*—not stingy. Pay for the meals when appropriate.

- *complimentary*—avoid being overly analytical. Be more of an encourager. Focus on being positive and never negative about your host's program or people even though you see things that could or should be improved.

Remember, you are not just there as an individual "getting in your two cents' worth" or "speaking your mind." You are an ambassador of good will on behalf of the entire board.

c. Discuss openly public information about your group. But when it comes to decisions on the board's behalf, remember your limits.

We recently heard about a young man who was representing his group. In one discussion (as the host perceived it), the young man committed the group to a considerable sum of money. When he returned he didn't mention this to the rest of his group. But shortly thereafter, to their surprise, the group received an invoice for several thousand dollars.

The representative had actually committed the group to this sum without authority. In this case, the man had given his word, and the group stood behind him at a great cost to their own budget. Remember your limits when you are committing or suggesting things on behalf of your group.

d. Take appropriate gifts of greeting, especially on international trips. Whenever you are visiting your international field offices, your mission fields, always take a small gift that cannot easily be obtained in that country, and represents your country or your community well.

Often the gift that makes the biggest impression is the one you would least expect to. When traveling internationally, it is amazing what a sack of American candy will do in a country where the American staff on the mission field can't find it to buy. It's a touch of home in a way that is extremely meaningful.

It doesn't have to be costly, but never go on trips empty-handed, especially when you are representing the group.

12. *Guest speakers*

When guest speakers address the group, the board has the responsibility to:

a. Pay adequately for the guest's expenses, including out-of-pocket expenses.

b. Give a tangible gift beyond dollars. Frequently we assume that a guest speaker is there to meet our agenda. We pay him what we think is an exorbitant amount of money. But, when we look back he has strengthened the lives of a lot of the people in our organization.

His honorarium (to be agreed upon ahead of the

service!) is an agreed fee, but not much "love, care
and appreciation" is expressed in dollars. Consider
going one step beyond and buying a little gift to say
thank you...a tangible gift that will be remembered
for years.

c. Assume your guest wants to stay in a quality hotel.
Often guest speakers are weary from travel and need
time alone to prepare. Staying in a member's home,
even though it may be interesting to the member and
cheaper for the organization, is disrespectful of the
guest speaker.

As two men who do a lot of traveling, we find it
very important (more important than those who do
not frequently travel may think) to have a hotel at
night. In homes of members, you may be kept up late
at night; you may be given food that doesn't agree
with you; you may have to sleep in beds that are
terribly uncomfortable; you may have grandfather
clocks gonging and dogs barking in the middle of the
night.

A word to the wise may be superfluous, but in this
case we will risk it.

d. Be a supportive encourager of the speaker. Many times
when a speaker comes into town, his audience is ini-
tially cold and indifferent. People tend to wait to see
whether they can trust the person—whether they will
accept him. Be an encourager from the beginning. If
you believe in the speaker enough to invite him, make
sure he feels warm, welcomed, and supported. Help
him feel at ease so he can give you his best.

e. Write a note a week later, thanking him for his
impact on the group and any personal impact he had
in your life.

f. Airport arrivals: Whenever a person is arriving or
leaving by air, consider the following:

(1) Have a senior-level leader in your organization meet the plane.

(2) Leave plenty of time so he doesn't have to rush!

(3) On the way back to the airport, encourage, recognize, and appreciate!

BY NOW you may be asking yourself, "Aren't you overstating what should be done in all this? Why are you taking this so seriously?" If that's your question, ask yourself this: "If I were in any of these situations, how would I want my fellow board members to treat me or my family?"

Even as a new board member, you can act appropriately regardless of what anyone around you does or does not do. Protocol is an area where the newest board member can contribute. Be an example of boardsmanship by taking the initiative in areas where more experienced board members may feel hesitant to express themselves.

Protocol can be summarized by a few basic principles:

a. You are representing the group, not yourself.

b. Do unto others as you would have them do unto you.

c. Don't wait for everybody else to act; you act in a gracious, loving, caring, sensitive manner even at the cost of your own comfort. That is protocol!

Section S
PUBLIC RELATIONS

ESSENCE: *Public relations is TELLING.*

TELL THE STORY of your organization so effectively that people naturally want to become involved with their time, energy and money.

Verley Sangster, the National Director of Urban Young Life in Denver, Colorado, tells how "everyone in Colorado is a part of the Chamber of Commerce." When every board member is acting like a one-person chamber of commerce for your organization, the excitement will spread rapidly and people will be attracted to you.

The senior executive and each staff member should be given "x" number of dollars a year to help create positive public relations on behalf of the organization.

How the community perceives your group is your "public image." You want to develop and maintain a positive public image. Your public image should not be created, however, but clarified. Tell honestly what your organization is doing and what needs it is meeting. It is dishonest to tell people you are something you are not, to project an image bigger than you really are.

Yet often an organization needs to clarify its community image because the image is outdated. As an organization grows stronger or more progressive, its letterhead, business cards, press releases and brochures should reflect the newness. Continuing to perpetuate the outdated image is inaccurate and, in a subtle sense, dishonest.

The following are a few considerations from a board perspective in the area of public relations:

1. *Designate a board spokesman for public relations.*

You may want to appoint a separate subcommittee of the board to help develop your public relations. You may also want to appoint a spokesman who will represent the board to the media. This person should be respected, articulate, a model of the board's values, intimately informed, and sensitive to what is and is not appropriate to disclose at a given moment. The usual spokesman for the group is the senior executive, since he is the most intimately familiar both with staff realities and the board's perspective. But before any crisis, be sure you have complete agreement between board and staff on "who is responsible for what" in public relations.

2. *Prepare a press kit to help news media find you.*

4s

Deliver a cleanly typed press kit to the newspaper, radio and TV stations. Include a one- or two-page news release, organizational brochure, any appropriate background information, photos and names, addresses and phone numbers of people the media can interview.

3. *Hold a press conference—when the occasion truly warrants it.*

Only when it is perfect timing and you have an announcement you feel is revolutionary or unusually newsworthy should you call a press conference. But even calling a press conference doesn't assure you will get coverage.

Cultivate the press consistently so they will be aware of who you are and what position you would take on a given subject. Assign one board person the responsibility of keeping the press informed on what is going on within your organization. Key contacts this person develops within the media will be extremely helpful when you do call your press conference.

4. *Honor people.*

Sincerely recognizing people who are contributing to the good of the community will result in positive public relations and possibly free media coverage of your organization.

Your board can honor people in ways that may be worthy of press coverage:

a. Express special appreciation for community, organizational or denominational leadership. Individualized computer letters could be signed by each member of the board. You could send out from five to a hundred letters a month to various people, appreciating their contribution at a local, regional, state, national or international level. An example of this might be a letter from your board expressing appreciation for the work of an anti-pornography committee or a pro-life group.

b. Plan a youth-honoring celebration, a banquet when you present letters signed by each board member, cash awards, or certificates or diplomas for a community youth organization or program.

c. Present belated awards for contributions not properly thanked in the past.

d. Posthumous awards to the family of deceased members or leaders within your organization.

e. Give special recognition to missionaries, field or international staff when they visit your church or organization.

f. Develop a "Silent Servant" award for people who serve behind the scenes and never expect recognition or appreciation by anyone. Send a two-paragraph letter signed by each board member to the maintenance staff, support staff, and volunteers.

g. Name a building after one of the organization's major contributors of time, energy or money. Plan a celebration and ceremony surrounding the dedication.

h. Honor the people who served on the building committee with a plaque displayed in the building.

i. Honor the senior executive who was in office when

the building was built, and who raised the majority of money. This can be done by a commemorative plaque in the building.

j. Honor large contributors of time, as well as money.

k. Recognize volunteers publicly by a letter signed by all the board, verbal recognition or flowers. Remember to praise the cooks who prepare refreshments for board meetings and other gatherings.

4s

It is nearly impossible to over-appreciate or over-honor people. Just be sure that the honor is sincere and consistent. Whenever one student is honored for "all A's," be sure every student with "all A's" is honored. Whenever you give an award to one person, make sure you give equivalent awards for equivalent accomplishments by other people. This will prevent hurt feelings. The need to render praise equally is a possible drawback to the honor system, but doing it fairly and consistently is well worth the effort.

5. *Annual report*

Many organizations use their annual report as both a financial report, and a public relations tool. Photographs, charts and diagrams can help create momentum within the organization, and with investors and donors.

The annual report is also an excellent tool to restate the needs, purposes and objectives for which the organization was founded. It provides continuing focus for the entire group, it can boost morale, and it can document progress annually.

You may want to publish an abbreviated report for mass distribution within your community, or within your larger constituent base.

6. *Ground-breaking ceremonies*

One reason a ground-breaking is newsworthy is that constructing buildings provides jobs for the community. A new major building actually changes the community by its presence. It represents a commitment on the part of the organization to investing in the community.

At a ground-breaking ceremony, it is often possible to get a picture of the board with key community officials for publication in the local paper. Provide mementos of the day, such as small brass shovels with inscriptions or mugs with the logo, date and occasion on them. Send a news release of the event not only to local news media, but also to denominational or organizational headquarters as well.

While the ground-breaking ceremony is important for public relations, it is also an excellent time to show appreciation to all the people who have contributed to the development of the project. Go out of your way to make an exhaustive list of the people who have helped. Give special honor to those who have made exceptional contributions.

7. Dedication of new buildings

A building dedication is another special way to thank all who have helped. Record and photograph speeches for the historic files. Invite all of your vendors, community leaders, tradesmen, the board and staff, and all volunteers involved with the project.

The board should budget enough money to give a memento of the day to the key people responsible for the building. This is a time to "do it right," not "get by."

Regard this as an opportunity to create good will and good public relations with all the people who are involved. A memento will be their tangible reminder of the satisfaction they have felt in helping create the building.

The dedication of a building marks a major milestone in the life of an organization and should be treated with respect. Organizational pride develops as the staff recognize the significance of the task they have accomplished together.

Section T
REPORTING

ESSENCE: *Are we on target?*

GETTING THE RIGHT FACTS paves the way for right decisions. Again quoting Peter Drucker: "Once the facts are clear, the decisions jump out at you." That is why a good system of reporting to the board is necessary.

4T

1. *A six-question reporting format suitable for all.*

It is important to have a single reporting system that everyone can use—the senior executive, the executive staff, the committee chairman, the chairman of special projects, and department heads. Below is a modified version of Masterplanning Group's six basic reporting questions, which give a broad overview of the results a person is achieving, as well as how he or she is doing personally.

Assuming your staff member has clear, approved goals, the six reporting questions are:

a. What *decisions* do you need from us to reach your goals?

b. What *problems* are keeping you from reaching your goals?

c. What new *plans* are you making?

d. What *progress* have you made?

e. On a scale of one to a hundred, how are you *personally*?

f. How can we *pray* for you?

2. *Financial reports*

(See Section L, "Managing Money," in Chapter Four.)

3. *Board minutes*

Board minutes should be prepared after each meeting and distributed to (and ready by) each member prior to the next meeting. This lets you avoid reading the minutes during the actual meeting.

The board minutes should include:

a. decisions that were made in the meeting
b. actions taken
c. clearly stated assignments and deadlines

If the minutes are clear and read ahead of time then it is simply a formality to approve them at the meeting in a three-second motion, saving everyone's time.

4. *Positive progress sheet*

Keep a list of the major milestones of your organization. Ask one person on the board or staff to be responsible to maintain this list. We tend to forget all of God's blessing.

When things are not going well, your progress list will be like a ray of sunshine cutting through the darkness. In Deuteronomy 8:2, God gave this command to Israel: "And you shall remember all the way which the Lord your God has led you..."

5. *Annual report*

Use your annual report as a reason for celebration for all the progress which has been made. State realistic problems where appropriate, but don't dwell on them. You can also make new friends by circulating widely your annual report, especially if it is a positive report.

Ask for reports from the senior executive, and give reports to other board members. Keep communicating!

Section U
RIGHT ATTITUDES

***ESSENCE*: When you have the right attitude...
people give you latitude**

DISPLAY THE PROPER ATTITUDES on the board and everyone will enjoy your success. Show the wrong attitudes, and they will enjoy your failure. This may not be Christian, but it is human. Your right attitudes make your entire board experience more pleasant for you and for everyone else.

4u

What are the proper attitudes that a board member should display? If you will work on these seven attitudes, everything else will tend to take care of itself:

1. *Focus on winning big, not just getting by.*

One way to distinguish between people who will be winners and losers in life is their life focus. People who are winners focus on "winning big" while losers focus on simply "getting by". As a board member, never focus on just getting by.

There are few things as pathetic as the whimper of a board member who asks timidly, "Is there a possibility we can get buy with only a three-percent raise in our executive staff salaries this year instead of ten percent?" Whenever you hear the words "get by," put a red light on in your mind and see if the board is dooming itself to failure by trying to just "get by".

There are few places in the history of boards where the "winning big" vs. "getting by" attitude shows up more quickly than in the stingy-generosity scale. In working with many top executives over the years we have found consistently that the really successful executives are generous, gracious men and women. They are committed to the fact that it is more blessed to give than to receive. Some organizations actually tithe all the money donated to them, to other organizations, as a part of their stewardship before God.

For only a few dollars an hour, you can double the effectiveness of an executive by providing a quality secretary. One of the places to have a "win big" attitude is to give adequate support staff to your executive team.

Dr. Henrietta Mears was the Christian Education Director at Hollywood Presbyterian Church in the 1950s. She is credited with having deeply influenced the lives of such leaders as Bill Bright, Billy Graham, and Richard Halverson. She is often quoted as having said, "Small dreams do not inflame the minds of men." As a board member, keep focused on "winning big." Don't let the board get bogged down in how you can "get by" by shaving a penny here and a penny there.

2. *Exhibit unconditional love...Give freedom to fail.*

One of the most restricting attitudes a board can display is one where every member must be perfect to be accepted by the group. A group has to give the individual member freedom to be less than perfect. Everyone needs to feel free to give his best ideas without fear of being looked down on or laughed at by the group.

People who differ from you aren't necessarily less; they're just different. On most subjects, a different opinion is not wrong, but simply different.

No one is perfect, but at the same time no one wants to fail. If you see a board member really failing in his attempts to be a part of a board, it is not because he wants to. He just doesn't know how to win. Give him some freedom to be less than perfect and listen to what he is trying to contribute.

3. *Display a "Servant-Leader" attitude.*

One of the most effective ways to make a difference in any group is to have an attitude which says, "I'm here to help you win," not "I'm here as an answer man—do what I say!" Focus on the group's agenda, what the group and its individuals want to do and where they want to go. "Do unto others as you would have them do unto you." Serve as you would want to be served.

4. *Retain a lifelong student's attitude.*

The best way to continue learning is to be teachable. Learn from everyone on the board, even the board member that seems to have very little to contribute. If you look carefully enough, he has much to teach.

Plan to peak in ten years. Say to yourself, "In ten years I'm going to be the best board member ever." Then on your birthday next year, move it up a year. When you're forty, you are ready to be fifty, and when you're sixty, you're just getting ready to be seventy. Plan to peak in ten years, but keep moving the ten years further ahead so you continue growing as a lifelong student.

The greatest leaders we have served with have also been the best students. Part of the reason they grow to so respected is that they have learned from so many people.

5. *Develop a family-level commitment to the group.*

The Apostle Paul wrote to his young protege, Timothy, "Do not sharply rebuke an older man, but rather appeal to him as a father, to the younger men as brothers, the older women as mothers, and the younger women as sisters, in all purity" (1 Timothy 5:1-2).

As board members, it is important to have a family-level commitment to other members, and especially new members. See them as mothers and fathers, young brothers and younger sisters. "Show them the ropes" like you hope someone would do for you. Treat them with the love and respect you would treat your own family, or would want someone to treat your father if he were invited onto a board.

6. *Develop critical thinking without a critical attitude.*

Dr. Bill Bright, founder and president of Campus Crusade for Christ, has insisted on the above theme throughout the Campus Crusade movement. Basically it means that you can disagree on issues, but don't be negative about another person. Look for ways to improve and strengthen an idea, instead of just shooting it down. Look for ways to encourage and appreciate one another, not to find fault.

7. *Keep a cooperative attitude.*

The late Francis Schaeffer advised, "Oppose wrong beginnings." Be willing to stand against everyone on issues which are unethical, illegal or immoral. At the same time, keep a serving, flexible, open, cooperative attitude on methods, preferences and procedures. Go along with the group if you don't have a lot of expertise and you see it isn't going to hurt them. Agree even though it may be three-percent less effective doing it their way than the way you would prefer. Going along will bring unity.

Competitiveness among peers may be praised in our culture, but it is not necessarily Christian. We are to serve our brother, not "beat" him.

As you display the proper attitudes, people will give you the freedom to fail...and they will be happy with your successes.

You may find that these seven attitudes do not come naturally to you. You may have to work at them. But remember: You're planning to peak in ten years.

Section V
RULES OF ORDER

***ESSENCE: Robert's Rules of Order are
a base—not a box.***

ROBERT'S RULES OF ORDER provide an excellent means of clear communications and a basis for concise note taking in recording the minutes of the meeting. If you have never led a meeting by Robert's Rules of Order, read carefully this section. You will quickly begin to feel the flow of motions, seconds, and "all-in-favors." It is really quite simple.

There are only a few procedural terms you will hear frequently in most board meetings. These terms are typically used by the chairman and there is a fairly predictable response coming from the board.

Here are the terms:

1. *Chairman asks, "Do I hear a motion?"*

A member responds, "I move that the following action be taken," which means, "I feel it is wise for us to move in this direction or to make this decision."

2. *Chairman asks, "Do I hear a second?"*

A member would answer, "Second" or "I second the motion," meaning, "I agree with this direction or decision."

3. *Chairman asks, "Discussion?"*

When you hear the chairman call for discussion, be sure to ask additional questions if you have doubts or concerns about the proposed direction or decision. And if you are definitely opposed or clearly disagree, say so. This is the time to either convince the rest of the group that your position is right, or to be convinced it isn't. So speak or forever hold your peace. If you don't speak now, be supportive later, because you had your chance.

4. *Chairman says, "All in favor, say, 'Aye.'"*

A ye" simply means, "I'm in favor of this direction or decision."

5. *Chairman also asks, "Opposed?"*

If you are opposed, simply say, "Opposed."

6. *Chairman says, "It is so moved," or "Carried."*

When (as is typically the case) everyone says "Aye" and no one says "Opposed," the motions made are "carried" or "so moved" and go into the official minutes. The minutes show the decisions and actions that are taken, along with the date of the vote.

The board on which you serve may use slightly different terms or a slightly different sequence, but this is the way most boards carry out their business. Most boards are not insistent on following the precise procedure in Robert's Rules of Order.

THIS CONCLUDES Chapter Four, and Step 4 in the Board Process. (Don't forget to mark your progress on page 13.) Understanding the Board Basics is foundational to effective board leadership. As you learn and apply these basic principles, you will maximize both your board and your leadership on the board.

The BOARD PROCESS Chart
For Boardroom Confidence

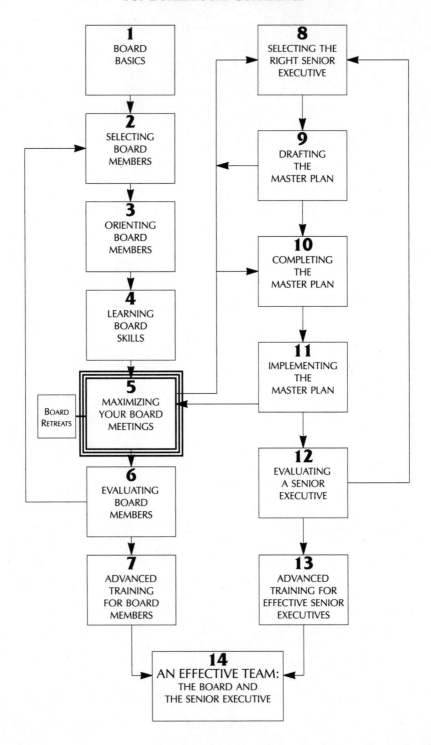

1 BOARD BASICS

2 SELECTING BOARD MEMBERS

3 ORIENTING BOARD MEMBERS

4 LEARNING BOARD SKILLS

5 MAXIMIZING YOUR BOARD MEETINGS

Board Retreats

6 EVALUATING BOARD MEMBERS

7 ADVANCED TRAINING FOR BOARD MEMBERS

8 SELECTING THE RIGHT SENIOR EXECUTIVE

9 DRAFTING THE MASTER PLAN

10 COMPLETING THE MASTER PLAN

11 IMPLEMENTING THE MASTER PLAN

12 EVALUATING A SENIOR EXECUTIVE

13 ADVANCED TRAINING FOR EFFECTIVE SENIOR EXECUTIVES

14 AN EFFECTIVE TEAM: THE BOARD AND THE SENIOR EXECUTIVE

5

MAXIMIZING YOUR BOARD MEETINGS

ESSENCE: The Big Four of board meetings are:
1. **The right board chairman**
2. **A clear agenda set well in advance**
3. **Strong, personal interaction**
4. **Simple, clear committee reports**

EVEN IF YOU serve on a board for forty years, keep looking for ways to improve the four basic factors listed above. As your meetings become more effective, you will progressively attract more qualified people to serve.

Let's first clarify a few assumptions:

ASSUMPTION 1: You have a clear Master Plan as a context for making decisions in your meetings. Typically, the Master Plan is drafted by the senior executive, then reviewed, refined, and approved by the board. Once you have a clear plan, your meetings will function far more smoothly.

ASSUMPTION 2: Two things need to be clearly and routinely established for your board meeting: (a) the time of starting and stopping, and (b) the place. If you can settle on a "same time, same place" plan, you won't be constantly wasting board time discussing when and where you will meet next.

ASSUMPTION 3: The size of the board is a variable that each organization must deal with in its own way. To decide what is right for you, you need to come to that delicate balance between (a) having enough people to gain objective perspectives and experienced input, and (b) not having so many that you can't function efficiently.

Some feel that a board should have from three people (the legal minimum) to eleven (an uneven number to avoid tie votes) as a maximum. Perhaps seven or less is better, since in larger groups, discussion can become a problem, causing meetings to run too long. Also, in larger groups it's harder to get everyone together regularly for meetings.

In research for this book we sent a questionnaire to many Christian leaders around the world. When asked what their greatest frustration was in serving on a board, the vast majority said, "The board meetings," then went on to cite one or more of four basic problems. Though worded differently, their concerns came out the same: (1) an ineffective chairperson; (2) the lack of a clear agenda in advance for necessary preparation; (3) the lack of personal relationships on the board; and (4) the lack of good, clear, simple, concise committee reports.

Twice as much frustration was expressed about these "big four" as all other concerns combined. Let's focus on how to maximize your board meetings by maximizing the big four.

Section A
SELECTING THE RIGHT CHAIRMAN

Essence: *Choose your chairman with extreme care...since ninety-five percent of a board meeting's effectiveness depends on the chairman.*

THE THREE KEYS to improving board meetings, according to George Underwood, president of Underwood Development Corporation in Dallas, are simple: "First, the right chairman; second, the right chairwoman; third, the right chairperson!"

George hits the nail on the head. When you have the right man or woman chairing the board, the right things happen. When you have the wrong person there, the wrong things happen. Finding the right person to chair the board is the critical move in a board's history.

Also critical, once the right chairman is in place, is the investment of training time and money to develop his or her leadership abilities.

In our questionnaire, the most frequently mentioned trait necessary for a chairman was the ability to stay with the agenda and time schedule. Also mentioned was the ability to summarize a lot of conversation quickly. The chairman must be a person committed to the ideal, who does not get caught up in defending a position. Rather than taking sides, he keeps looking at the best in both sides of an issue to come to an ideal solution. He must be committed to investing the time and energy needed to do his homework on all issues.

You'll find a sample board chairman profile in the Appendix. When the time comes to select a chairman, you may want to adapt our profile to your own use, making it a tailored profile for the kind of man or woman your particular board needs . Present that profile as a possible guideline for selecting your next chairman.

Section B
THE AGENDA

ESSENCE: K.I.S.S. (Keep It Simple, Servant)

Ideally your board meetings will consist of brief reports, brief but thorough discussion, and decisions. With a clear agenda distributed ahead of time (along with study papers and any other proper homework), the board meeting is primarily a forum for discussing and approving recommendations.

The chairman and the senior executive typically get together to create the agenda for the coming board meeting. All the suggestions we heard from respondents to our board questionnaire could be summarized in this guideline: "Keep the agenda short and simple by screening carefully what goes on it." The board agenda should include only the items the board must decide upon. Most operational decisions should be made on the executive staff level.

A pre-agenda checklist for the chairman and senior executive to consider might include questions such as these, to help screen out unnecessary agenda items: Can this item be resolved at a staff level? Do we have enough information to bring this item to the board? Is the timing right? Should this be referred to a committee instead of the board?

Send the agenda to each board member about ten days before the meeting—late enough so it won't get laid aside, early enough so research and thought can be given to the agenda items. We recommend that any reference material related to an agenda item be sent with the agenda. This material might include: a background statement giving reasons for the item; statistics; projected costs; and projected impact on the organization of a proposed decision. When everyone does his homework, meetings can end on time.

Another way to shorten the agenda is to combine routine items on the agenda in a block vote. The agenda reflects which items are recommended as a block vote. Instead of voting on each issue individually, the chairman simply says,

"Do I hear a motion to accept the decisions suggested in the block voting section of the agenda?" If he gets enough "ayes," all items are passed at once without further discussion. Obviously, if someone has a question about an item, that one issue would be discussed separately.

Another key to effective meetings is a definite time limit for each part of the agenda, and a clearly agreed upon adjournment time for meetings. Stick to the agenda and keep moving the discussion toward clear, concise decisions.

5

Section C
INCREASING PERSONAL INTERACTION

ESSENCE: *Friends discuss; strangers argue.*

THE MORE your board members become friends the more effective the board will be. Attendence and morale at board meetings will increase, and discussions will require less time. Do all you can personally to promote friendships among board members.

We've found the following two questions to be helpful in promoting friendly conversation in the boardroom:

1. "What is the most meaningful thing that has happened to you since our last time together?" When you ask this question you will hear mostly positive, happy responses, but in some cases you will be touched by someone's very deep hurt. Warm, supportive relationships are developed through this kind of interaction.

2. "Between now and the next time we meet, how can we, as a board, be praying for you?" This question helps a member share anxieties and concerns. He

will be encouraged to know fellow board members are praying with him about these needs.

By asking these two questions, you are developing the social, burden-sharing side of your board relationships. As members begin praying for each other and giving thanks together for key achievements, the group will bond at a personal level.

As mentioned earlier, the role of refreshments in a board meeting can hardly be overstated. The refreshment break is a good time for humor, team spirit and relieving tension.

A note of warning: Don't allow yourself to be a negative kidder. Barbs, gibes, and put-downs, even when said in jest, are often harmful to people and to social relationships. Some have grown up in an environment where it was acceptable to see how defensive or embarrassed they could make someone by their clever comments. But as a mature Christian leader, you may find that what was acceptable in the past should be nonexistent now. The Scriptures teach us to think on the positive things and not to let coarse jesting be a part of our conversation. Negative kidding can be a destructive dynamic, destroying the interpersonal trust and security within the group.

Some leaders see the personal interaction at the beginning of a board meeting—the key personal questions, the spiritual sharing—as only optional. We don't. People need to express their personal agendas before dealing with the group agenda. If you don't deal with the personal pressures first, you will have resistance and hidden agendas coming up during the meeting. And without personal dialogue at the beginning, you can expect a later adjournment.

Section D
REPORTS FROM COMMITTEES

ESSENCE: *If you can't give a report in five minutes or less...keep working on it.*

HOMEWORK IS ESPECIALLY CRITICAL when you are a member of one of the board's committees. Concentrate on visualizing your report with charts, graphs, or diagrams. Communicate the simple essence of your information or recommendation. Work at summarizing your research. In short, keep your report brief! Be a model of clear, concise reporting. Use your homework time to compress your report, thus saving the board time. When everyone concentrates on preparing short reports, you will have time to discuss those weighty issues which should not be shortened.

Staff reports should be limited to one page each, and each report given a specific, limited time frame.

5

Section E
REDUCING THE MOST FREQUENT BOARD MEETING FRUSTRATIONS

<u>ESSENCE</u>: *Board meetings don't have to last until 2:00 A.M.*

IN THE SURVEYS we conducted, we've found nine key points of frequent frustration with board meetings. Concentrate on helping your board avoid them.

1. *Digressing from the agenda into low-priority items*

Be sensitive to your own personal involvement in the meeting. Too much coffee or sugar can stimulate active conversation that may not be relevant to the agenda. One side comment may result in humorous chatter that produces verbal "fog" in the meeting. Watch that you are not guilty of contributing to this kind of distraction. Before you speak, ask yourself, "Is what I'm about to say on track, or is it a tangent?"

2. *Not doing the necessary homework*

Never come to a board meeting unprepared. Always set aside time on your calendar to make sure you get your homework done in advance. If you come unprepared, admit it up front. The admission of failure will keep you from doing it too many times in the future.

Help young, inexperienced members see the value of doing their homework so they don't waste group time. With a loving attitude, say, "Let me show you the ropes," or "I'd like to help you be a strong contributor in our meetings." Then show them how to prepare.

3. *Failing to adequately plan the agenda*

The chairman and senior executive must plan the agenda a minimum of two weeks before the board meeting. Create and review an agenda checklist and make sure you cover only the necessary items.

Get a clear, simple agenda in the mail at least one week in advance of the meeting.

4. *Interfering with staff operations*

One of the things you should avoid at board meetings is getting involved in the day-to-day operations or administration of the organization—unless invited to do so by the senior executive.

On financial questions, as a rule of thumb discuss only those matters that are of a sufficient dollar amount to demand your time and counsel. One way to decide if an issue is the proper size for a board to deal with would be to set an arbitrary figure of "x" percent of your budget. Don't waste the board's time on anything less than that.

For example, let's say you decide any amount less than five percent of your annual *variable* budget (the variable budget in most organizations is about fifteen percent of the total budget) is a staff decision not requiring the board's consideration. If your organization's total budget amounts to $1,000,000 a year, with a variable budget (fifteen percent) of $150,000, then unless an item represents at least five percent of that—or $7,500—the board should not be discussing it.

5. *Unqualified board members who are lacking in vision and motivation*

If you are unmotivated, resign. It will be a relief both for you and the board. If you question your contribution, ask the senior executive to help you see why you should or should not stay.

Only talk when you feel certain you have something

helpful to say. If you find that you never talk, that you have nothing to contribute to the group—consider resigning.

This book is written to help you know how to succeed as a board member. To the extent you feel unqualified or into something "way over your head," be fair to yourself and the rest of the board. Seriously consider resignation, and discuss it with your senior executive.

6. *Focusing most of the meeting on money*

As chairman, prepare the financial reports (graphs, charts, summaries) so they take twenty minutes or less. Set a time limit on the amount of time you discuss financial issues, unless there is a major problem. Instead, spend most of your time talking about major policy issues or problems and opportunities related to ministry or service.

7. *Making decisions without seeing the big picture*

Ask yourself, "Am I thinking of my special interest in my favorite department; or am I thinking about what is best for the entire group?" Remember to keep a clear overview of direction, organization and finances. Think at a board level, not at a middle-management level.

8. *Not having available a record of previous decisions*

It is important for each board member to have a board reference notebook which organizes his thinking about the past, present, and future. In *The Effective Board*, Cyril Houle recommends the following components be included in a board notebook:

    a. a description of the organization
    b. the organization's constitution
    c. articles of incorporation
    d. bylaws

e. an annual schedule for the board
f. a list of board members with addresses and telephone numbers
g. a list of committees, with a statement of the function and membership of each
h. a statement of policies and procedures
i. an organizational chart of the staff
j. the current budget
k. a statement of any controlling legal provisions or major commitments to outside groups

You'll also want to include a copy of all minutes and reports. After each meeting, the board's secretary should record:

a. any constitutional or bylaw changes or additions
b. any policy changes or additions
c. all decisions made
d. a list of action items to be followed up, along with the names of people responsible for doing them and deadline dates

The vestry (board) of St. James Episcopal Church in Newport Beach, California, tape-records every vestry meeting for future reference. One advantage of this practice is that a group can reconstruct key discussions which may not have seemed critical at the time.

9. *Poor chairmanship*

If you find the chairman is doing a poor job, try to help him improve. If *you* are the chairman, seek the help of other people who can help you lead more effectively.

As a chairman, you may want to attend board meetings with other groups similar to your own. This "speed modeling" trip will help you become aware of optional agenda formats; ways of handling conflicts and discussions; and many other ways to improve your effectiveness as a board chairman.

Section F
RETREATS—ONE OF THE MOST EFFECTIVE BOARD-BUILDING STRATEGIES

> ESSENCE: **At board retreats, concentrate
> on these two areas:**
> 1. **Building personal relationships**
> 2. **Clarifying the organizational context—**
>   - **directional**
>   - **organizational**
>   - **financial**

STRANGE AS IT SEEMS, retreating is one of the best ways to progress, especially in the case of board retreats. A retreat can help you establish social relationships, and help you develop a clear context in the form of a Master Plan for the future.

A retreat gives temporary freedom from time constraints, which is probably the most frequent board frustration. Although it must be organized properly to maximize the time available, a retreat allows you more discussion of major aspects of the organization (such as the purpose statement). In a typical board meeting this would not be the case.

1. *Preparing for a board retreat*

Your first step in preparing for a board retreat is to review a pre-retreat checklist. Here are sample questions to help you focus on the essentials:

  a. Are we planning to "win" at this retereat, or just "get by"?

  b. Are we planning to meet needs, or just to maintain our present condition?

c. Are we being servant-leaders?

d. Are we providing opportunity for emotional support of one another as board members—time for personal sharing, and building supportive relationships?

e. Are we providing spiritual development?

f. What three measurable things do we actually want to accomplish at the retreat?

g. What pre-retreat assignments should we make to maximize our time?

h. What location will be most conducive to our purpose for the retreat?

i. What dates for holding the retreat are best for all our board members?

Organizing the board retreat and coordinating all the details can be a major undertaking. Ed Trenner, a consulting associate of Masterplanning Group, has written a helpful resource called *Checklist —For Planning Any Special Event or Retreat*. This 300-point checklist can help protect you from forgetting an important detail and also provide many helpful ideas to maximize your retreat.

2. *Typical retreat frustrations*

Even though a retreat may run from Friday night through Sunday morning, the time always seem surprisingly short. One typical frustration comes from having unrealistic expectations about what can be accomplished in so short a time.

Another frustration is the lack of agreement on terms used in the planning process. Often when boards go on a planning retreat, they spend half the time there trying to define the process and terms they will use. This is extremely frustrating because you come back from a working weekend with no plans, dooming you to continue operating just as you have in the past.

The confusion of roles between the senior executive and the board can be another source of frustration on a planning retreat. If you let the senior executive and executive staff draft the Master Plan, then let the board review it, refine it, and approve it on the weekend.

3. *Succeeding at retreats*

If you focus your retreats on the following primary areas, you will make tremendous progress as a board—and stimulate the organization's growth:

a. Encourage one another with honor, recognition, and appreciation.

b. Remember the positive things that have actually happened—the group's milestones.

c. Clarify the organizational context for the year by presenting the senior executive's draft of the Master Plan, and having the board review, refine, and approve it.

d. Build relationships for the coming year.

4. *Having objective, outside counsel at your retreats*

The advantages of having outside counsel present at your board planning retreats include these:

a. An outside consultant brings objectivity plus a commitment to help you identify and reach your goals.

b. A consultant uses a single planning process which he can take the board through.

One frequent question asked by boards is: "Can't one of our board members—one who has expertise in planning —lead us through the planning process more effectively than an outsider?" Consider these points:

a. The planning expert in your group could quite probably help the planning team of another group far more effectively than he could help his own, simply because of his objectivity with another group.

b. Often a person who does planning for a large corporation finds it difficult to adjust to the processes and tools of a smaller, nonprofit organization.

c. If you have two or three "planning experts" on your board, you probably also have two or three different planning processes, none of which may be compatible. Frequently a competitive spirit ensues.

d. A group values the counsel it pays for. The board member who would insist on this principle at work may think it is not true in a nonprofit or church setting, but we have found it to be true everywhere.

With adequate preparation and clear focus on what you want to achieve, your board retreats can be fun, productive, fulfilling times for the entire group.

HAVING COMPLETED Step 5 (mark your progress on page 13), you are now ready to take up the topic of Evaluating Board Members.

The BOARD PROCESS Chart
For Boardroom Confidence

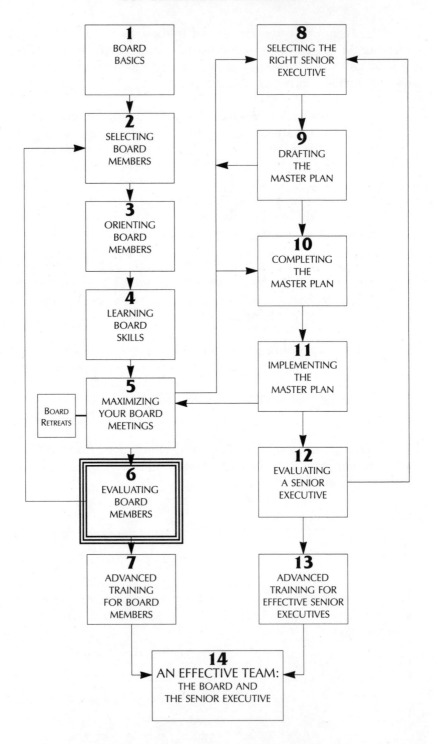

6

EVALUATING BOARD MEMBERS

**ESSENCE:** "Here to help you succeed" is the right attitude in evaluation.

WHEN YOU EVALUATE a board member or are being evaluated as a board member, focus on the question: "How can each of us be more personally effective in helping the group succeed?" When you have established an environment of acceptance and mutual concern for one another's leadership development, evaluation will greatly strengthen everyone.

Evaluating people is rarely comfortable. Although it is not an easy assignment, it can be rewarding as you watch each board member strengthened and the quality of your board improve. Accept the fact that there will always be a natural anxiety present when evaluating or being evaluated by your peers. Yet if the evaluation happens in an environment of acceptance, love and support, it can be a freeing experience.

Each board member needs to feel he is making a positive contribution. He needs to know he is meeting the expectations of the group, not just taking up space at the table. He needs to feel wanted by the group. Each board member knows where he stands with the board.

The only way most will know how they are doing as a board member is if they are told at an annual evaluation time. If they are not told, they will go through the year wondering if they are making any difference, perhaps thinking they should resign. Yet knowing the kind of contribution you are making helps you to be even more productive. This is the value of evaluation.

Section A
THE EVALUATION PROCESS

ESSENCE: Every person deserves to know...
* *how he is perceived by his peers.*
* *where he is strong.*
* *where he needs to grow.*

A STANDARD EVALUATION PROCESS provides a systematic, orderly way of helping people know where we feel they are strong and where we feel they need to grow in order to make an even more significant contribution.

When each person understands that everyone on the board and staff is going through the same evaluation process, resistance tends to be reduced.

Section B
THE BOARD EVALUATION SHEET

ESSENCE: *An evaluation sheet is a comprehensive way to get personal without being offensive.*

WHEN A BOARD MEMBER is being evaluated, the board chairman, the senior executive, and the board member himself should independently complete an evaluation sheet like the sample in the Appendix—which you may want to change if necessary so that it works best for you.

Such three-way evaluations usually come to the same conclusions, making easier the resulting decision. In the case where all three people agree that the member should stay on the board, the decision is automatic that he stays. If all three feel the person should leave, that decision is also automatic decision. Where there is not a three-way agreement, you simply discuss each area of concern until you reach clear agreement.

A strong, three-way agreement will result in stronger relationships, commitment, and resolve.

When a person leaves the board for a term or so and comes back with any differences resolved, he is usually a much greater contributor to the board. Conversely, if a person stays on the board when he should really leave for a term, he frequently is the source of frustration, tension, occasional anger, bitterness, and deadlock. This is particularly true on a board that requires unanimous agreement for decision making.

Section C
RECOGNITION FOR BOARD SERVICE

ESSENCE: *Ninety percent of all volunteers are inadequately recognized for their service. (It's no wonder they don't want to re-enlist.)*

RECOGNIZE EACH PERSON'S contribution and you'll discover that people want to work for you. The following are proven ways to express recognition for service rendered:

1. A board dinner or reception in his honor.

2. A notebook with letters of appreciation from all the board members and significant constituents.

3. An engraved wall or desk plaque.

4. Airline tickets to a favorite destination.

5. A page in the organization's "Hall of Fame" notebook. (A notebook with pictures of honored board and staff; brief descriptions of each person and the accomplishments during their term; personalized comments about each one—some humorous, some appreciative.)

6. A personal gift of appropriate worth and meaning to the board member.

It is important to note that recognition of volunteer service is always inadequate for the service rendered. One useful rule is that end-of-term gifts—or the amounts spent on public recognition—should be approximately $10 per year of service for board members. For example, a retiring member is given a $30 recognition if he has served for three years; if he has served ten years, the board should be comfortable investing $100 in his recognition.

Over a period of ten years a board member may have

spent thousands of hours on subcommittees and projects helping your group achieve its goals. Don't become stingy or cheap when the member retires—retire him with honor. (See Section R on "Protocol" in Chapter Four.)

A time of evaluation provides you an opportunity to recognize members who have made significant contributions to the board. Don't miss this opportunity to build stronger ties with your members and to hold up ideals to which all can aspire. Through the process of careful, sensitive, honest evaluation, your entire group will begin to develop greater loyalties to one another and a stronger commitment to your board.

The BOARD PROCESS Chart
FOR BOARDROOM CONFIDENCE

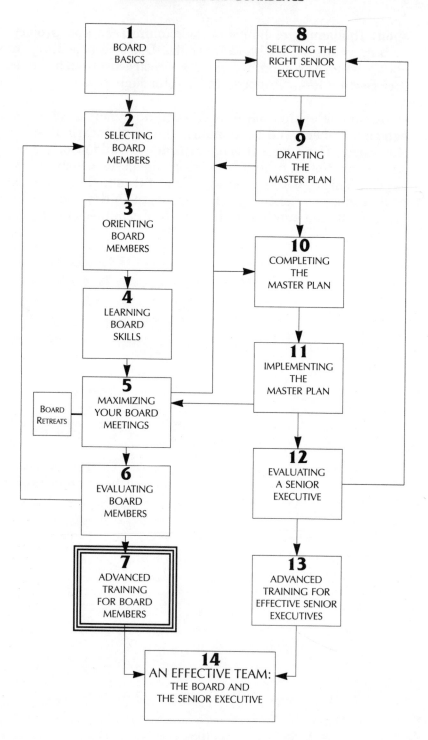

7

ADVANCED TRAINING
FOR BOARD MEMBERS

ESSENCE: **_Every organizational unit is a direct reflection of the leadership it has been given, for good or bad. Therefore, focus on developing leaders, especially among board members._**

CONCENTRATE ON DEVELOPING LEADERS at every level of the organization. In the church setting, your future board members are now in your new member classes. You need to prepare them to serve some day.

Two almost equal tragedies hamper organizational development. One is being in a situation without opportunity. The second is being in a situation with many opportunities but no leaders trained to take advantage of them.

Section A
SEMINARS AND LIBRARIES

ESSENCE: Your board would do well to allocate three to five percent of the organization's variable income to leadership development.

INSIST THAT CAREFUL ATTENTION be given to the development of your executive staff and board. Make leadership development a part of your annual budget. When your board members start growing in their leadership ability, you'll notice positive attitudes and a fresh sense of growth in the group.

Areas of leadership development of particular concern to executive staff and board members include:

1. decision making
2. marketing
3. Master Planning
4. money management
5. project management
6. people skill development
7. problem solving
8. public relations
9. questioning
10. fund raising

When you know of a high-quality seminar addressing any of these topics, pass the information on to the staff and board. Also consider sponsoring a seminar on a particular topic.

A reference library of books, audio and video tapes, and seminar notes on any of these areas of leadership will be a tremendous resource in the development of your team.

Section B
SPEED MODELING TRIPS

ESSENCE: *One speed modeling trip can teach you more than three months of experience at home.*

A "speed modeling trip" is a field trip to an organization similar to your own—though ideally, the organization is slightly larger or more fully developed than your own. If the organization has programs you do not have but would like to initiate, you can benefit greatly by observing them actually work.

Have you ever noticed how differently people learn? Some learn by reading, some by doing. Almost everyone can learn well by active observation. Once your board or sub-committee has seen what others have actually made work, they have a far greater understanding of what they can and cannot do.

You may also want to plan speed modeling trips to field offices and branches to pick up new ideas. International visits can have the dual advantage of combining a learning experience with a "verifying" trip—to see what you have heard about for years. This is particularly important to an international ministry depending on donors from other countries. People tend to put their money where their eyes have been.

Section C
BRINGING IN OUTSIDE RESOURCE PEOPLE

***ESSENCE:** An outside resource person can often do more in two hours to move a group in the right direction than the board can do on its own in fifty hours of discussion.*

ALL BOARDS OCCASIONALLY need to be stimulated, motivated, and challenged to think and act in new ways. Whenever an outside resource person is available, ask yourself if the board should be exposed to him. Whether you agree with the resource person or not, the board grows as it discusses and clarifies what he tells you, and you'll be more unified as a result of your common encounter with a stimulating person from the outside.

It may be appropriate for such a resource person to speak not only to the board, but also to your constituents or staff.

Be alert to learn about experts and consultants who are visiting another organization in your community similar to yours.

You may want to invite a specialist from a nearby university or consulting firm to speak to your group.

Section D
TRAINING THE CHAIRMAN—
AND FUTURE CHAIRMEN

ESSENCE: If your board invests ten percent
of its entire training budget on the board chairman
and on the two or three people who are
likely to be chairmen in the future—
you won't be wasting money.

PUT EXTRA TRAINING DOLLARS into the chairman, as well as into the potential chairmen of the future. The stronger your chairman, the stronger the board. Your meetings become better, committees more effective, and morale higher.

In selecting your next chairman, it would be wise to have your board continue to work on describing the profile of the ideal chairman. (In the Appendix you will find a sample board chairman profile. You will want to add, subtract and change this profile to fit your organizational needs.)

When the time comes to choose a chairman from the two or three people you have been training, the decision should be fairly obvious, based on your completed profile. If possible, let the chairman-elect work closely with the current chairman for a period of a year to gain confidence in his ability to lead.

The board chairman should establish a system to encourage the board and staff to develop their leadership skills on a consistent basis.

VIEW ADVANCED BOARD TRAINING as a necessity, not a luxury. If your group is to continue to grow, board members must be able to contribute in an increasingly effective way.

171

The BOARD PROCESS Chart
For Boardroom Confidence

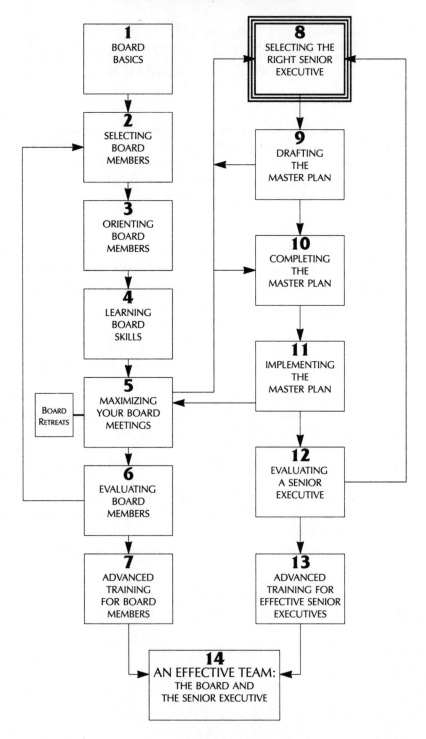

1 BOARD BASICS

2 SELECTING BOARD MEMBERS

3 ORIENTING BOARD MEMBERS

4 LEARNING BOARD SKILLS

BOARD RETREATS

5 MAXIMIZING YOUR BOARD MEETINGS

6 EVALUATING BOARD MEMBERS

7 ADVANCED TRAINING FOR BOARD MEMBERS

8 SELECTING THE RIGHT SENIOR EXECUTIVE

9 DRAFTING THE MASTER PLAN

10 COMPLETING THE MASTER PLAN

11 IMPLEMENTING THE MASTER PLAN

12 EVALUATING A SENIOR EXECUTIVE

13 ADVANCED TRAINING FOR EFFECTIVE SENIOR EXECUTIVES

14 AN EFFECTIVE TEAM: THE BOARD AND THE SENIOR EXECUTIVE

8

SELECTING THE RIGHT SENIOR EXECUTIVE

ESSENCE: **_Every organizational unit is a direct reflection of the leadership it has been given, for good or for bad._**

SELECTING THE RIGHT senior executive is the single most important board responsibility. It is the one decision that, more than any other, makes all else work effectively. By selecting the right senior executive you save yourself a hundred headaches that would result if you made a wrong choice.

When you hire a senior executive, you are hiring a directional leader. Be thorough and complete in the selection process before the invitation is extended. Be diligent to pray for God's wisdom in choosing a leader for your organization.

Section A
THE SELECTION PROCESS

**ESSENCE: *The higher the placement, the more
process-dependent and consistent you want to stay.***

ONE OF THE MOST COSTLY mistakes you can make is not following an established process in selecting executive leadership. Too often the board gets excited about a possible senior
executive and skips a few of the process steps, only to find a
year or two later that he is not what he appeared to be.

The following is a checklist from Masterplanning Group
for "Recruiting Executive Level Staff." After going through the
full process, you can relax knowing you did everything possible to hire the right person and screen out the wrong ones:

1. Consult Master Plan/organizational chart
2. Appoint search committee (optional)
3. Create position focus/profile for position
4. Get budget approval for position
5. Announce position opening
6. Receive résumés...establish file
7. Send basic information packet to candidates
8. Contact references...

For each person on final list of candidates:
9. First interview...evaluate
10. Create psychological profile
11. Second interview...evaluate
12. Third interview...evaluate
13. Trial period (if possible)
14. Final committee discussion and decision

For the person chosen:
15. Make offer in writing, then acknowledge acceptance
16. Prepare for arrival
17. Orientation
18. Evaluation: *Winner!*

Section B
INTERVIEWING CANDIDATES

ESSENCE: *The answers that tell you most about a candidate are his answers to "what if" questions.*

SPECIALIZE IN ASKING "what if "questions when candidates come to visit. Prepare and use them this way:

1. Think of the most difficult, high-pressure situation this person could possibly (yet realistically) face, and turn it into a question.

2. Ask how he or she would handle this situation.

3. Evaluate the person's answer to determine if this is the way you would want the situation handled.

8

Here are examples of effective questions:

What would you do (and how would you do it) IF...

- You received your monthly financial report and saw that income for the month was thirty percent less than projected in the budget.

- You received a phone call from one of your largest clients (donors, supporters, buyers), who said he will end their relationship with our organization unless a certain person on your staff is fired.

- You found that your most trusted staff person has been talking negatively behind your back.

- Your most loyal staff member was not producing adequate results, and your board says to fire him or her. (The "How would you do it?" portion of the answer to this question could be particularly revealing.)

- Two extremely strong members of your team (board member, staff, or volunteer) took very opposing views on the direction your team should go.

- One of the board members "went around you" and instructed one of your staff to carry out a certain task in his job.

- On your first day of work in your new position here, you were told that your budget and staff must be reduced by fifty percent.

- On your first day here, you found that your team was in a depression...a deep slump.

- On your first day here, you learned that you are expected to double the size of the organization in two years.

- After an enjoyable first year in your new position here, another organization offered you a similar position with a twenty-percent higher salary.

Adapt these questions to your own situation, and be sure to ask the standard recruiting questions as well. Once your questions explore the assumptions the candidate is making, you can predict his future behavior. People base their decisions and actions on their assumptions (The Masterplanning Group publication *Art of Asking* provides further discussion of how assumptions and questions affect the decision making process.)

Section C
INVENTORIES

ESSENCE: Inventories clarify and verify...and occasionally mislead.

AN INVENTORY—a personality or temperament analysis—of a candidate for senior executive can clarify any areas your interview missed, and verify areas where you are uncomfortable trusting your instincts. If you remember that inventories are not absolute truth, they can be extremely helpful, especially in the early stages of the screening process.

As you interview your candidate, administer two or three back-up inventories such as the Role Preference Inventory, the Myers-Briggs, or the Taylor-Johnson Temperament Analysis to verify and clarify your interviewing conclusions.

Assuming you stay with the basic selection process and continue to refine it as you use it, the chances of making a mistake are greatly reduced. Remember R.C. Sproul's advice: "The best time to fire a person is when you don't hire him."

8

The BOARD PROCESS Chart
For Boardroom Confidence

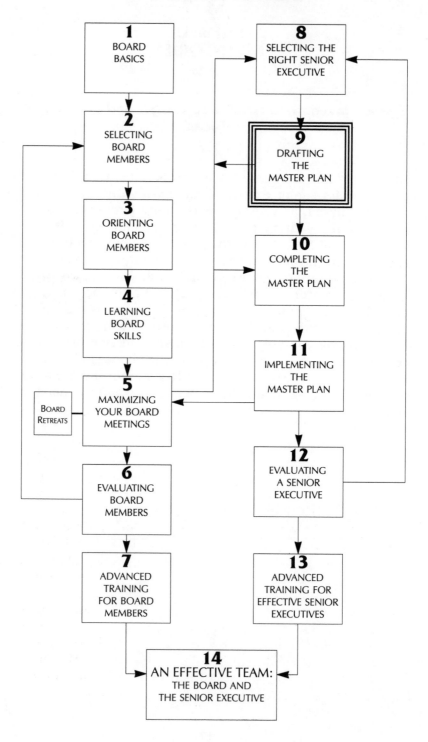

9

DRAFTING THE MASTER PLAN

ESSENCE: **_Without a clear Master Plan, everyone has the feeling of being part of the same band, but playing different music._**

DEVELOPING ANY ORGANIZATION without a Master Plan is like running a race without a finish line. You have no points of reference. You have no direction, no track to run on, and no way of marking your progress

As we've mentioned, a Master Plan is a written statement of the group's assumptions about its direction, organization, and resources. A Master Plan allows everyone to work together toward common goals. It is essential before team harmony can really begin to develop.

Occasionally you may question whether planning is in conflict with faith. You reason: "If today has enough trouble of its own and life is but a vapor that appears a short time and then is gone, then perhaps planning is futile. Besides, God is sovereign. He will have His way regardless."

Actually, planning is an evidence of faith, not a contradiction to it. As you plan a building, you are expressing faith that God will bring people to fill it. God instructs us to count the cost before building. That's planning. He tells us to "redeem the time," to make the most of opportunities. That requires thoughtful planning and discipline.

Read James 4:13-15. When you plan (and James assumes you will plan), you ought to say, "If the Lord wills." You don't plan to do something regardless of what God says; you plan something with a heart that is sensitive and submissive to God's approval or disapproval.

Section A
THE SENIOR EXECUTIVE'S PART

*ESSENCE: **Make the most of the senior executive's in-depth knowledge of the organization.***

IF THE SENIOR EXECUTIVE is able to write the first draft of a Master Plan, you have the best of both worlds: The senior executive has the broadest and deepest experience in the organization, and he is the person the organization will ultimately reflect. You have the concentrated energy of one person looking at the big picture of the organization. He is making sure all the pieces are covered. (Later you will also gain from the board's wisdom as board members review, refine, and approve the Master Plan. But while the senior executive may spend ten hours drafting the plan, the board may need only one hour to do its part.)

A senior executive whose leadership style is directional does not claim to be the final authority in creating the Master Plan (as would a dictatorial leader). The directional leader simply says, "I will serve the group's best interest by doing the first draft. My first draft of the Master Plan is always 'in pencil,' ready for refinement by others. In specialty areas I will solicit as much input as possible from executive staff, and I will allow the board to review it, refine it, and approve it.."

At the same time, the directional leader doesn't just sit around waiting for a committee to decide what the Master Plan should look like. This would typically lead only to confusion.

(The content and process of Master Planning is described in Section L of Chapter Four.)

9

Section B
GETTING STAFF INPUT AS NEEDED

ESSENCE: Build an organization from
the bottom up—and from the top down!—
by giving the staff goal-ownership in
the Master Plan

YOUR ORGANIZATION'S STAFF needs to have input in the Master Plan if they are to feel "goal-ownership". Your senior executive needs their extensive practical wisdom. Insist that he obtain staff input on the Master Plan before the board sees it. It will save everyone a great deal of time.

The board should ask for a Master Plan draft on which the senior executive and his staff are in agreement. Once you have a Master Plan, everyone—board, senior executive, and staff—will be making the same assumptions about the organization's direction, its organizational structure, its cash and budget policies, and its reporting, evaluation, and refinement systems. You will all be playing the same music.

This sensitivity of the board to the staff's involvement reflects the board's total commitment to the staff in these areas: to help the staff achieve its goal; to help develop leadership in the staff; and to maintain a supportive relationship with the staff. It is entirely proper for a board member to go to lunch with staff members occasionally and to be an encouragement to them. You may also ask permission from the senior executive for what is known as a "skip evaluation". This is a time when the board asks to see an executive staff member, to communicate with him or her directly rather than going through the senior executive. The purpose of the meeting is evaluation and encouragement.

It is often difficult to maintain strong personal relationships board members and executive staff, so go out of your way to make it happen. You will have to work at it, but it is worth it.

Be careful, at the same time, not to allow the staff

member to "end run" the senior executive and get you to champion his cause with the board. Remain loyal to, and work through, the senior executive, while maintaining friendly relationships with executive staff as well.

9

The BOARD PROCESS Chart
FOR BOARDROOM CONFIDENCE

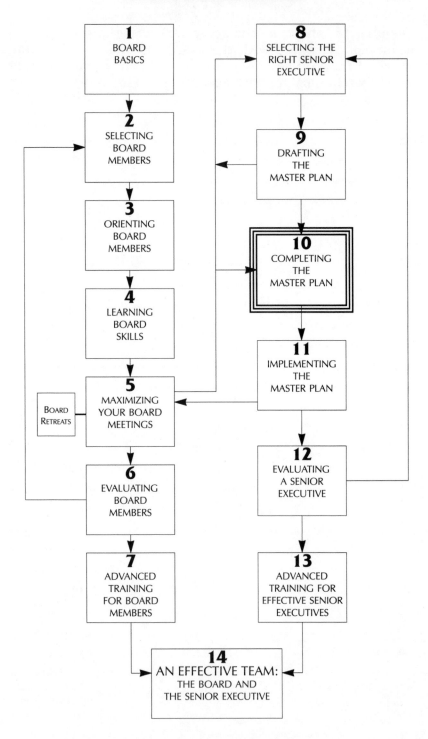

COMPLETING THE MASTER PLAN

Section A
REVIEWING THE MASTER PLAN

Essence: The "red, yellow and green" process may not be technical, but it sure is practical.

As THE BOARD looks over the Master Plan drafted (with staff input) by the senior executive, you can apply the "red, yellow and green" process to help you do your review work. This process isn't sophisticated or technical, but it works wonders in helping you review long lists of proposed directions and actions.

With this method the entire board can review in minutes the organization's directional statement in the Master Plan. This is the way it works: Each major point in the directional statement is reviewed and given a red, yellow, or green value by each board member. Red is opposition; yellow is caution; green is approval. The chairman reads the first point on the directional paper and asks, "Do you respond with red, yellow, or green?" If each board member says "green," meaning, "I feel very comfortable with that," you simply continue to the next point, making note of any items which receive even a single red or yellow from any board member .

When you've worked your way through the entire directional statement, go back and discuss those points that
received any yellow ratings (or a mixture of red and green).
For each point, talk about your questions and reservations
until you feel comfortable as a group in making the unanimous rating for that point either all-green or all-red.

You can safely expect the process to be a confirming one.
If your board gives its responses to fifty points, you're likely to
have only five or ten that fail to receive all green ratings from
the group. And most often, after discussion, many of the reds
and yellows are upgraded to green as board members have
their questions answered.

Section B
REFINING THE MASTER PLAN

*ESSENCE: "Without consultation, plans
are frustrated, but with many counselors
they succeed" (Proverbs 15:22).*

THE REFINEMENT STEP requires thoughtful counsel from all
board members. Each member has a lifetime of experience
and accumulated wisdom to contribute. Guard against
being a rubber-stamp board, approving everything presented
to you. At the same time, avoid raising questions simply to
be a devil's advocate.

Section C
APPROVING THE MASTER PLAN

ESSENCE: **Don't stop with simply giving approval to the staff's Master Plan... go on to appreciation and accolades!**

IF THE STAFF does a shoddy job of preparing the Master Plan, send them back to the drawing boards. If they do a great job of planning, praise them profusely. Next year they will do even better.

Here is a simple equation we have found helpful: When you combine the word "track" (meaning "a clear plan"), and "action," you get "traction." If your senior executive and executive staff don't have a clear track to run on (an approved plan), but they take a lot of action, the result is a lot of wheel-spinning. If they have a track, but take no action, the result is just as disappointing. But when they have a good track and then take action, your organization has the *traction* to achieve major accomplishments.

By coming to a complete agreement about the Master Plan on all three leadership levels, you achieve a feeling of deep unity that few groups experience. You'll see also that all three levels interacting on the plan produced a result far better than any one of the levels could have alone.

Section D
TRACKING THE MASTER PLAN

Essence: *"Are we on track?"*

ONCE YOUR Master Plan is in place, keep asking your senior executive the six reporting questions (they're listed in Section T of Chapter Four) to make sure your plan gets implemented. The six-question tracking system keeps you from getting bogged down in too many details.

The BOARD PROCESS Chart
For Boardroom Confidence

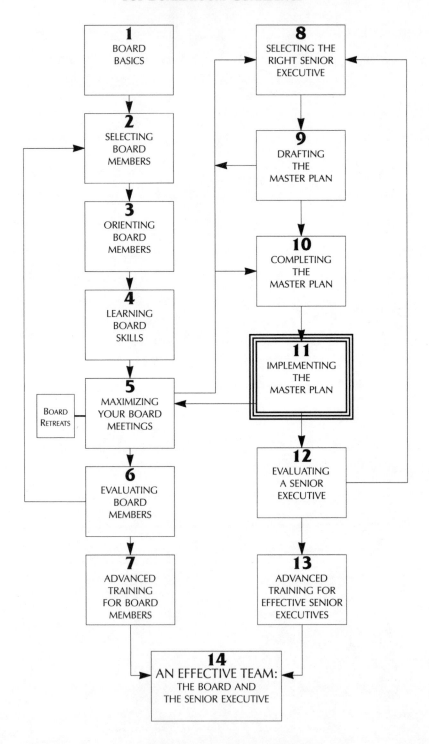

11

IMPLEMENTING THE MASTER PLAN

ESSENCE: If the senior executive will report to you, you can help him; if he won't, your hands are tied. So insist on clear goals and consistent reports.

ONCE THE SENIOR EXECUTIVE has begun implementing the Master Plan and is reporting regularly to the board, your role becomes that of an encourager, decision maker, and problem solver.

Insist that the senior executive report to the board on a regular basis using the same six questions used in staff reporting. (See the list in Section T of Chapter Four.) This regular report will protect you from having to admit, "I really don't know what's going on." When you know what the senior executive is struggling with, you can help him succeed—which is one of your primary board responsibilities.

The BOARD PROCESS Chart
For Boardroom Confidence

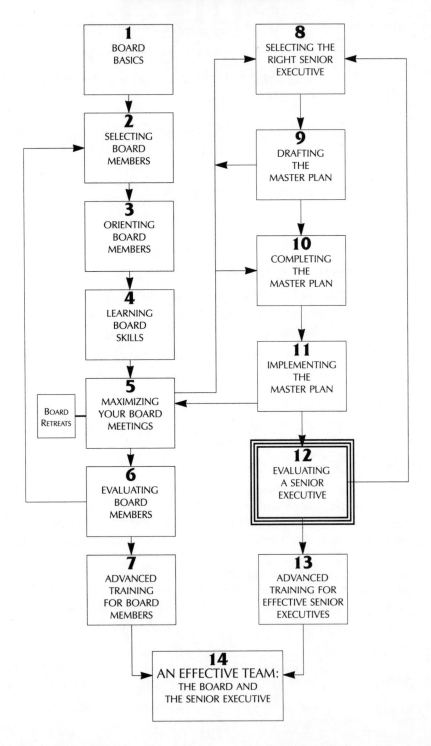

EVALUATING A SENIOR EXECUTIVE

Section A
WHY EVALUATE?

ESSENCE: *Evaluation precedes growth and improvement*

YOU OWE your senior executive a realistic, honest evaluation once a year. Your annual evaluation process gives you an appropriate, honorable way to express praise and frustration. Without such a process, gossip and negative comments become a major temptation.

Remember too that rather than resisting an annual evaluation, a senior executive often looks forward to it—especially if the board is also being evaluated, and if he knows his own evaluation will be done in a loving, caring way.

Peter Drucker, the father of modern management, made this point at a recent retreat we attended: "All one *can* measure is performance; and all one *should* measure is performance." You can't judge a man's achievements based on his dreams. He continued, "One can measure the performance of a man only against specific performance expectations."

If you are going to evaluate the senior executive, clear goals for him are essential, as well as a clear position focus sheet.

Drucker made another observation often overlooked in an organization: "Subordinates, especially bright, young, and ambitious ones, tend to mold themselves after a forceful boss. There is, therefore, nothing more corrupting and more destructive in an organization than a forceful but basically corrupt executive. Such a man might well operate effectively on his own; even within an organization, he might be tolerable if denied all power over others. But in a position of power within an organization, he destroys."

As you evaluate the senior executive, then, you should have in mind the future of the organization and the quality of his influence on those working under him.

Keep in mind also the senior executive's performance is a rather big picture. Reports and records reflect his effectiveness, but they give only a partial view of the situation. Use conversations and extensive personal observation to help complete your perspective on the executive's effectiveness.

When an evaluation confirms the board's strong sense of confidence in the senior executive, it is good to give him a vote of confidence publicly on an annual basis, as well as an annual pay increase. Additionally, after he has completed an appropriate number of years in service, consider granting him a sabbatical for study or for taking advantage of special growth opportunities. It can last from three to twelve months, with full compensation continuing during that time.

Section B
COMPENSATION CONSIDERATIONS

ESSENCE: *If your senior executive is struggling to "get by" in his personal and family finances, he will rarely be able to help the board keep its focus on "succeeding in a major way."*

OFTEN THE DIFFERENCE between "winning" and "getting by" for the senior executive is a cost of less than one percent of the organization's income. But not taking care of the senior executive adequately affects ninety-nine percent of the group's identity and effectiveness. Once your senior executive is "winning" in his personal finances, he can release his entire energy and potential to helping the group succeed—a great energy release for a relatively few dollars.

The financial compensation to the senior executive is critical to his effectiveness as your directional leader. You may want to appoint a confidential subcommittee of two or three people to consider the senior executive's compensation package. There are at least ten levels of consideration in how much a senior executive should be compensated:

1. time in position
2. value and level of the position
3. record of performance
4. cost of living
5. bonus
6. stock sharing
7. pension and profit sharing
8. housing allowance
9. expense account, especially for personal growth and organizational entertaining
10. honorariums

12

Note: Verbally expressing appreciation is critical to a senior executive's motivation, but it cannot take the place of compensation.

Section C
WHEN THE JOB ISN'T GETTING DONE

ESSENCE: *When a senior executive is not doing what you want, you have more than the two options of (1) "gritting your teeth" or (2) firing him.*

WHEN A SENIOR EXECUTIVE is not meeting the board's written expectations, ask these questions:

Why is the job not being done right?

Is it lack of training?
Is it lack of motivation?
Is it lack of experience?
Is it lack of ability?
Is it lack of clear assignment?

Answers to these questions can guide you in helping the senior executive become a more productive leader. (*Leading with Wisdom*, a notebook/cassette series available from Masterplanning Group, contains hundreds of principles and questions to help you in evaluating and encouraging your executive leadership.)

The cruelest response you can make as a board member is to "let it slide" when you see a senior executive struggling. Once the board acts in the best interest of both the senior executive and the group, everyone can relax and focus on future goals, rather than on the weaknesses of the senior executive.

If your later evaluations indicate that he continues to struggle in his position, the following options should be considered. If they are weighted carefully and thoroughly, the right decision should become obvious to you.

1. *Granting a leave of absence*

Do not release a person from the senior executive's position, or accept his resignation, when he is just feeling tired and worn out. Instead, suggest a leave of absence to restore his energy level and preserve his leadership promise.

2. *Setting a conditional continuation in the position*

If there are certain corrections the senior executive needs to make, you can allow him to stay in his position pending the corrections. This should be understood as a temporary situation for a stated number of months, during which his performance will be carefully watched and evaluated. When the necessary changes have taken place, give your executive a green light for the future. If there is no improvement, you can then accept the resignation.

3. *Accepting his resignation, or releasing him*

Probably the hardest assignment in all the world is to release a key executive—especially to do it in a Christian way.

One crucial guideline in doing it well is to mentally separate the person from the position. Remain committed to and supportive of the person while, at the same time, pointing out that he did not meet a standard of excellence or a specific, measurable criterion within the organization. Tell him that, based on this failure to meet expectations, you believe it is time for him to leave and move on to something that fits him more comfortably. Make it clear that you nonetheless respect and love him, and are deeply committed to his well being.

When you appropriately "fire" someone from a task at which he is failing, you are actually releasing him from failure and "firing him up" with the excitement of the new future that such a release represents.

12

Section D
WHEN THE SENIOR EXECUTIVE LEAVES

ESSENCE: The way you treat departing senior executives tells everyone what your board is really made of. So use the occasion to show them!

WHEN THE SENIOR EXECUTIVE leaves, the board should return in the same measure the generosity the senior executive has shown the group. Here's where you want to "shine big," insisting on proper honor for the retiring senior executive.

Team morale in the organization either slumps or skyrockets when a senior executive leaves, depending on the way you treat a departing executive. When he leaves with appropriate honor, everyone feels great and the unspoken message to all staff is: "This is the class with which you will be treated some day."

Board actions to be taken when a senior executive leaves include these:

1. Appoint a trusted person as interim leader

2. Mark the calendar to communicate regularly with the search committee's progress

3. Reassure the staff that they still have a clear Master Plan. (During a two-year period when it had no senior pastor, the Evangelical Free Church of Huntington Beach, California, actually grew—because its leaders had a clear Master Plan.)

4. Make the board more visible with reassurance and reports to the group as a whole.

You will also want to put together a "check-out" checklist. When a person resigns he is given a checklist similar to the orientation checklist he received when he "checked in". The list should include questions about locations of materials, records, names of key contacts, what materials you want returned (books, tapes, keys, credit cards)—anything he knows that you will want to know.

12

The BOARD PROCESS Chart
For Boardroom Confidence

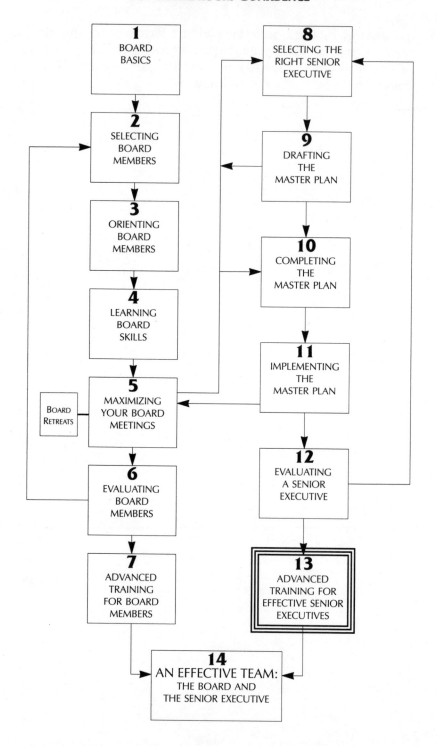

ADVANCED TRAINING
FOR SENIOR EXECUTIVES

ESSENCE: _Every organization is a direct reflection of the leadership it has been given. Build your senior executive, and you build the entire organization._

YOU WILL FIND that building your senior executive strengthens and stimulates him, broadens his perspective, and keeps him in place longer. A person who is growing rarely leaves an organization. When a senior executive feels stagnant he becomes susceptible to the urge of accepting an outside offer.

Opportunities for the senior executive's advanced training are similar to those for the board member. Consider speed modeling trips to meet with executives at other organizations. Consider advanced education through a university or seminary. Consider sending him to any of the numerous seminars that are given on a wide range of leadership topics that can help build your senior executive. International travel can be another consideration.

An important aspect of advanced training is budget. An annual amount set aside for his development will allow him to attend seminars or classes and to put together a leadership library. Remember, investing in your senior executive is actually an investment in the organization.

Another way to encourage growth in your senior executive is to allow him to perform services outside the group. For example, the New Covenant Church of God in Middletown, Ohio, allows and encourages its senior pastor, Claude Robold, to be a consulting associate with Masterplanning Group so he can help other groups strengthen their programs. His church sees it as an educational and developmental experience for him as he shares with others the principles he has used to help make their church successful. It is another form of advanced training.

The real challenge is to look for ways of helping your senior executive keep stretching. As you allow him to continues developing, he will stay with you and be more productive for your organization.

The BOARD PROCESS Chart
For Boardroom Confidence

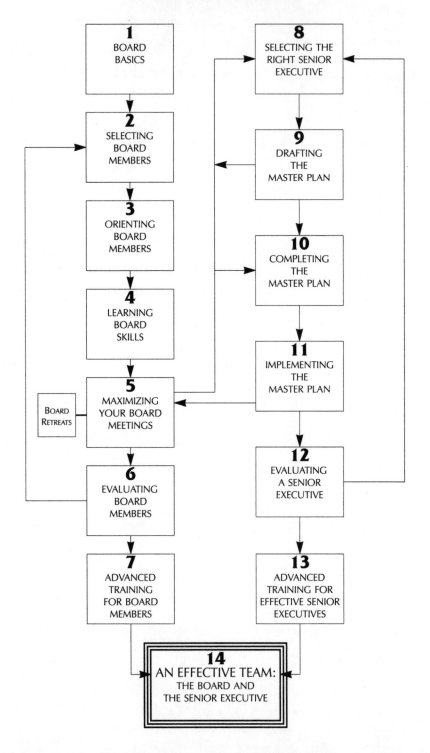

1 BOARD BASICS

2 SELECTING BOARD MEMBERS

3 ORIENTING BOARD MEMBERS

4 LEARNING BOARD SKILLS

5 MAXIMIZING YOUR BOARD MEETINGS

BOARD RETREATS

6 EVALUATING BOARD MEMBERS

7 ADVANCED TRAINING FOR BOARD MEMBERS

8 SELECTING THE RIGHT SENIOR EXECUTIVE

9 DRAFTING THE MASTER PLAN

10 COMPLETING THE MASTER PLAN

11 IMPLEMENTING THE MASTER PLAN

12 EVALUATING A SENIOR EXECUTIVE

13 ADVANCED TRAINING FOR EFFECTIVE SENIOR EXECUTIVES

14 AN EFFECTIVE TEAM: THE BOARD AND THE SENIOR EXECUTIVE

14

AN EFFECTIVE TEAM
THE BOARD AND
THE SENIOR EXECUTIVE

ESSENCE: _They'll know you're Christians by your three-level love—not by your milestones._

Do EVERYTHING in your power to create a loving, caring, supportive attitude at all three levels of leadership in your organization. (Everything goes better when people truly respect and care for one another.)

Ask the senior executive to have lunch with a different board member once a month at the organization's expense. This can enhance the board's relationship with him. He can also meet with a different board member each month in a one-day retreat, where these questions could be asked:

1. In what aspect of your work do you find the most personal fulfillment—and why?

2. What are you planning to do this year that you have never done before?

3. What tools, equipment, facilities or personnel could help you most in maximizing your potential?

4. What areas of your work cause you the most personal stress and frustration, and why?

5. What is the most meaningful thing you have experienced in the past year?

6. In what ways do you most want to grow personally in the coming year, and how can I help you grow in these areas?

7. What is the most helpful thing for me to know about you, to truly understand "the real you"?

8. What three people do you most enjoy being with, and why?

9. What do you do just to have fun?

10. To help you grow this year, what courses would you like to take? What books would you like to read? What experiences would you like to have?

11. What are your dreams for the next five to ten years?

12. What do you consider your three greatest strengths, and how can I help you maximize them?

13. What roadblocks do you feel are holding you back in any aspect of your life, and how can I help you remove them?

14. Are there any personal problems you would like to talk about with me?

15. Is there any unresolved difficulty in your life which you've wanted to speak to me about, but haven't known just how to approach the subject?

16. What is the single area of your life you would most like me to join you in praying about this year?

17. What do I do that demotivates you?

18. What do I do that motivates you?

19. In what area would you like to see me grow this year? Is this an area you feel you could help me in, and can you suggest others who could help me?

20. What have I forgotten to ask you that would be most helpful to me in understanding who you are and who you would like to become—or where you are going and how I can help you the most in getting there?

Another effective means of bonding the senior executive and the board together is for the senior executive to visit the board member's work place and observe him in his own environment. This provides an opportunity for the executive to become familiar with the pains and pressures as well as the rewards and fulfillments of the board member's work.

The senior executive should invite board members to staff picnics, Christmas parties, and other organizational activities. This helps build trust between the board and staff rather than the progressive distrust that often develops in a relationship in which there is not constant interaction.

14

CONCLUSION

BOARDROOM CONFIDENCE is a reference book to help you develop not only confidence in the boardroom, but also lifelong leadership confidence.

Maximize your board tenure! Develop lifelong friendships. Grow, stretch, contribute, have fun, be significant ...enjoy!

As you make the most of your board experience and continue gaining in boardroom effectiveness, if you should come to a roadblock for which a five-minute telephone conversation with one of us would be helpful, give one of us a quick call:

Bobb: (714) 495-8850
Ted: (818) 357-7979

If we don't have an answer we can frequently refer you to someone who does.

IN THE NEXT THIRTY DAYS

We encourage you to do three specific things in the next thirty days:

1. Apply something specific from this book to your board responsibilities.

2. On an 8½" by 11" sheet of paper, make a one-page

summary of the principles you have learned in this book (write small). Then put the sheet in your board notebook for quick reference.

3. Go through your organizational chart or your address book and decide who else would benefit from reading BOARDROOM CONFIDENCE.

We close with one of Bobb's personal experiences:

THE ELEPHANT STORY

It was eleven o'clock one Friday night. I was sound asleep when the phone rang. On the other end was my friend Duane Pederson, founder and editor of the *Hollywood Free Paper.* "How would you like to go to Tucson tomorrow?"

"Tucson?" I groaned. "What in the world would we do in Tucson?"

"My friend Bobby Yerkes has a circus playing in Tucson tomorrow and I'd like to just go down, get away, clear the cobwebs, and work the circus with him. We'll move some props, have a good time, and be back by ten o'clock tomorrow night."

In my mind Duane's words called up boyhood dreams about running away with the circus. It didn't take me long to agree to go.

The next morning at seven our jet lifted off the runway at Los Angeles International Airport, headed for Tucson. When we got there, it was a hot, dusty, windy day at the fairgrounds where the circus was playing.

We moved props from one of the three rings to the next, helped in any way we could, and generally got dusty, dirty, tired and hungry.

During one of the breaks I started chatting with a man who trained animals for Hollywood movies. "How is it that you can stake down a 10-ton elephant with the same size stake you use for this little fellow?" I asked. (The "little fellow" weighed 300 pounds.)

"It's easy when you know two things: Elephants really do have great memories, but they really aren't very smart. When they're babies, we stake them down. They try to tug away from the stake maybe ten thousand times before they realize that they can't possibly get away. At that point, their 'elephant memory' takes over and they remember for the rest of their lives that they can't get away from the stake."

We humans are sometimes like elephants. When we're teenagers we hear someone saying about us, "He's not very handsome...she's not a good thinker...he'll never be a good leader," and ZAP, it drives a stake into our minds. Often as adults we still are held back by some inaccurate one-sentence "stake" put in our minds when we were younger.

Our prayer is that *BOARDROOM CONFIDENCE* will help you pull up some of the "stakes" holding you back. Today you are an adult capable of much more than even you realize. You are more mature and capable than you were even twelve months ago, and next year you'll be able to do things you can't do today.

Let's pull up those stakes—and go on together to true confidence in the boardroom!

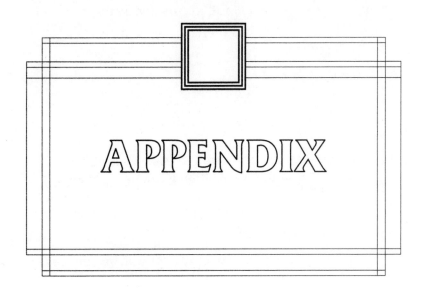

APPENDIX

**Resources for Your
Boardroom Confidence**

CONTENTS

Board Membership

Ten Questions to Ask Yourself BEFORE Agreeing to Serve on the Board

*(As you think about your answers,
record your thoughts in the space provided.)*

1. What will be expected of me as a responsible board member?

2. Can I make the time available to effectively serve on the board—to do the necessary homework, to attend meetings and retreats, etc.?

3. What qualifies me to serve on this board? What would I bring to the board in terms of my experience, abilities, interests, resources, and relationships?

4. How long of a commitment am I willing to make to this organization?

5. Do I really believe in the organization?

6. Do I feel truly supportive of the organization's senior executive and the executive staff?

7. Is my spouse supportive of my serving on this board?

8. Are there any hidden things in my life that would disqualify me from serving, if they were known?

9. Why should I *not* serve?

10. Do I sense God's leading in this decision?

Leadership Commitment
(A Sample Pledge)

Knowing that God has spoken clearly in His Word concerning the character and responsibility of a leader, I do solemnly commit myself to God and to the leadership board of this church to do the following:

1. I will seek to maintain a close, intimate walk with the Lord by regularly spending time alone with Him in His Word and in prayer.

2. I will be a diligent student of God's Word.

3. I will endeavor to walk continually in the Spirit.

4. I will pray regularly for those who serve with me as board members, for the pastor of the church we serve, and for the pastor's staff.

5. I will pray regularly for the ministry of the church.

6. I will give ten percent of my income to the work of the Lord through this church.

7. I will faithfully attend all meetings of the board, unless I am hindered from doing so by a compelling reason such as illness or necessary travel. When unable to attend, I will notify the board chairman in advance, if possible, of the reason for my absence.

8. I will prepare for each board meeting by doing my homework and by submitting myself anew and afresh to the Holy Spirit.

9. By the power of the Holy Spirit, I will refrain from expressing negative attitudes through criticism and complaint. Instead, I will be positive and encouraging, endeavoring to maintain the unity of the Spirit in the bond of peace.

10. I will maintain an open and teachable attitude.

I have studied these statements of commitment and have prayed over them, and I believe God would have me serve the board as a member according to these standards.

SIGNATURE:_____

DATE:_____

PROFILE:
The Board Chairman

*The personal traits and skills listed here are
necessary for any man or woman to effectively
fulfill the responsibilities of chairing a board.
Use this list to help you choose carefully the
right person to lead your board.*

He or she:

- Is a natural encourager

- Has the respect of the board members

- Has a good *feel* for the constituents or congregation;
  is able to sense their needs and their response to
  board decisions

- Is able to sense and care for people who are hurting
  or not being heard

- Has superior communication skills

- Has a proven record of staying with the agenda and
  time schedule

- Has a proven track record in negotiating differences

- Is able to keep several programs working at the same
  time

- Has a wide range of exposure to the organization and understands how it works

- Has a deep appreciation of and commitment to the organization, its purpose, its staff, and its activities

- Meets the character and moral qualifications of the organization; has a good reputation among the board members and constituents

- Is willing and able to give the time and energy necessary to prepare and lead the board

Question Lists

30 Questions to Ask Yourself BEFORE Making Major Decisions

NOTE: Not every question in this list will help you in every situation. This is simply a checklist to help you keep from overlooking important considerations before confirming and carrying out major decisions.

The thirty questions here can save you many hours, and perhaps thousands of dollars.

As you weigh your answers, use the space below each question to jot down your thoughts.

1. At its essence—in one sentence—what is the decision we are really facing? What is the "bottom, bottom line"?

2. What facts should we have before we can make this decision with total confidence?

3. What trends, changes, or problems are behind the need for this change? How long will these continue to be a factor?

4. Are we dealing with a cause or a symptom? A means or an end?

5. What does the Bible say about this situation?

6. Am I thinking about this situation with a clear head, or am I fatigued to the point that I shouldn't be making major decisions?

7. What would the ideal solution be in this situation?

8. Should we seek outside counsel in making this decision?

9. What are the hidden agendas that are "pushing" for a decision in this situation? Why do "we" or "they" want a change? What is the source of the emotional fuel that is driving this decision?

10. If I had to decide in the next two minutes...what decision would I make, and why?

11. What decision would I expect each of my three most respected advisers to favor in this situation?

12. Can an overall decision in this situation be broken up into parts, with "sub-decisions" made at a few "go/no go" points along the way?

13. What are the key assumptions in our thinking that underlie the decision we're leaning toward? What do we assume it will really cost? What do we assume will be its real benefits?

14. Who?...What?...When?...Where?...Why?...How?... How much?

15. Have we given ourselves twenty-four hours to let this decision settle in our minds?

16. What difference will this decision make a year from now? Five years? twenty years? A hundred years?

17. Is this decision consistent with our values in the past, or does it mark a change in direction or standards?

18. How will this decision affect our overall Master Plan? Will it sidetrack us?

19. Will this decision help to maximize our key strengths?

20. Have we verified what the results have been for others who have made a similar decision in similar circumstances? Have we checked this thoroughly?

21. How do we really *feel* about this decision?

22. Is this the decision we would make if our budget was twice as large as it is? Half as large? Five times as large? One-tenth as large? Is it the same decision we would make if we had twice as many staff members? Half as many?

23. What would happen if we did *not* carry out this decision?

24. If we didn't carry it out, what would be the best three alternative decisions?

25. Is this the best timing for carrying out this decision? If not now, why? And when?

26. Is this decision truly appropriate in scope and size to the situation we face? Are we possibly hunting an elephant with a BB gun, or a rabbit with a cannon?

27. As I pray about this decision, and look at it from God's perspective, do I have a sense of peace about it?

28. How do our families feel about this decision? How will it affect them?

29. What questions still linger in our minds? What aspects of the situation will not be resolved or solved by this decision?

30. Should we write a policy about this decision to guide us in similar situations in the future?

Brainstorming Questions

For a new IDEA (or project, or plan, or program)—

1. What is the ESSENCE of the idea, expressed in one word?

   One sentence?

   One paragraph?

2. What is the ultimate "blue-sky" POTENTIAL of this idea?

3. What are the five biggest things that could keep us from realizing the full potential? How can each of these ROADBLOCKS be cleared away?

4. What are our five most fundamental ASSUMPTIONS behind the idea?

5. What changes would we make in the idea if we knew we had three years to carry it out?

    Three months?

    Three days?

    Three hours?

    Three minutes?

6. Where could this idea be ten years from now?

    Twenty-five years?

    A hundred years?

7. What could or would we do if this idea were a hundred times more successful than we had planned?

8. Which part of the idea deserves the most funding?

9. Which part of the idea could most easily be dropped and not missed?

For overall organizational strategy—

1. What are our five most fundamental ASSUMPTIONS about what we do?

2. WHY are we doing what we're doing?

3. What could we do if our STAFF was twice as large as it is now?

   Five times larger?

   Cut in half?

4. What could we do if our current BUDGET was twice as large?

   Five times larger?

   Cut in half?

5. How could we DOUBLE our income and CUT IN HALF our costs?

6. What are our five greatest STRENGTHS, and how can we maximize them?

7. What are our five greatest OPPORTUNITIES, and how can we make the most of them?

8. If we had to START OVER, what would we do differently?

9. What would it take for us to be NUMBER ONE in our field of endeavor?

10. What are the top ten GOALS we could accomplish in the next ten years?

11. What are the top ten ways we could make an IMPACT on the world around us in the next ten years?

12. In our most idealistic perspective...what can our TEAM be like ten years from now?

Idea Sorter Questions

Questions to help you sort out the best ideas
after a time of brainstorming

1. Which idea best meets our needs?

2. Which idea has the greatest potential?

3. Which idea would be most cost-effective in the long
   run?

4. Which idea best fits our overall Master Plan?

5. Which idea is the most realistic for our staff today? Do
   we have the right project leader?

6. Which idea could help us WIN rather than just "get
   by"?

7. Which idea has the lowest front-end risk?

8. Which idea would be the most practical on a day-to-
   day basis?

9. Which idea is most worth taking a risk for?

10. In which idea would I be most willing to invest my own
    money?

Questions to ask about the "best" idea—

1. What additional facts are needed before we can properly refine and implement the idea?

2. What are the most likely obstacles we would face in carrying it out?

3. What is the feeling about this idea among those who bear the most responsibility for our organization's success?

4. Where would we get the money to successfully carry out this idea—to "do it right"?

5. Why have others failed in trying similar ideas in the past?

6. What are the side effects—good or bad—of carrying out this idea?

7. Is the timing right for implementing this idea?

8. Is the idea protectible, patentable, copyrightable?

9. Would we have to stop something else we are now doing to carry out this idea?

10. How can we test the idea before committing major resources to it?

Recruitment

Candidate Interview

A Sample Form

Candidate's Name: Phone:

Address:

BEFORE THE VISIT: Make sure you have all the materials you'll need—
- *Doctrinal statement*
- *Position focus sheet, or other appropriate description*
- *Biblical qualifications*
- *Statement of commitment*

HOME VISIT:

1. Membership and Attendence

    Are you a member of the church?

    How long have you been attending?

    How often do you attend Sunday morning services?

        Sunday evening services?

2. Salvation

    Have you come to the place in your spiritual life where you know *for certain* that if you died today you would go to heaven?

    Suppose you did die and stood before God, and He said, "Why should I let you into heaven?" What would you say?

Describe briefly the circumstances surrounding your conversion.

3. Spiritual Life

   How do you feel about your present relationship with the Lord?

   What has the Lord been teaching you lately?

   Have you ever read through the entire Bible?

   What is the most significant training you have received for living the Christian life?

   Are you willing to receive additional training?

4. Marriage and Family

   Spouse's name:

   How long have you been married?

   Have either of you been divorced? (If so, give basic facts here:)

   How would you describe the quality of your marriage relationship?

How would you describe the spiritual condition of your spouse?

Do you have children? (If so, list names and ages:)

How would you describe the spiritual condition of your children?

5. Personal Finances

    How stable are you financially?

6. Employment

    Where are you employed, and for how long have you worked there?

    What is your job?

    Are you a supervisor or manager? (If so, tell how many people you are responsible for, and give the size of the annual budget you are responsible for)

    How do you feel about your work?

    How would you evaluate your job performance?

    What is your boss's name and phone number?

7. Church Leadership Experience

What church leadership experience have you had?

How well do you feel you carried out your responsibilities?

What present church leadership responsibilities do you have?

8. Giving

What percent of your income do you give to the work of the Lord?

What percent of your income do you give directly to your own church?

9. Doctrinal Beliefs

(Have the person read your Doctrinal Statement, and sign it if he or she endorses it. Record questions or comments here.)

10. Position Focus Sheet or Job Description

(Read over this carefully with the candidate. Record questions or comments here.)

11. Biblical Qualifications

(Discuss the list with the candidate. Leave the list with him, and ask him to do a self-evaluation after you've gone.)

12. Statement of Commitment

(Go over this together)

Question for spouse: Do you feel your husband (or wife) should accept this position? Why do you feel this way?

(Close the interview with prayer.)

AFTER THE HOME VISIT

1. Contact the candidate's employer and ask these questions:

    How would you evaluate (candidate's name) as an employee?

    How would you rate him with respect to integrity and honesty?

    How would you rate him in the area of diligence?

2. Contact other references, and record your findings here:

3. Conduct a second (and possibly third) interview with the candidate, and record your observations here:

4. As a final decision nears, make sure you have in the candidate's file (a) his self-evaluation as per the position's biblical qualifications, and (b) the Doctrinal Statement and Statement of Commitment, both signed by the candidate.

Position Focus Sheet: Explanation and Instructions

As a recruitment and job placement tool, the position focus sheet can be used to clearly define any paid or volunteer position in your organization. It is designed to be adapted by YOU for YOUR purposes. View it as a starting point, not a comprehensive, all-inclusive form.

Person Assigned—A name is written here after someone actually agrees to be responsible for the position. The line should be blank when you show the "Position Focus Sheet" to position candidates.

Effective Date—This is the specific date when the person will begin assuming responsibility for the position.

1. Position Title—Be specific and complete: "Coordinator of...," "Assistant to...," "Director of ...," etc.

2. Purpose—State in one sentence, in simple words, why the position is necessary.

3. Reports To—Who is responsible to see that this person succeeds in the assigned position, and to answer his or her questions? *Each position should report directly to only one person.*

4. Relates Closely With—Who are the other team members with whom this person will work?

5. Responsible For—If this position is a supervising role, who will the person be responsible for supervising?

6. Continuing Responsibilities—The routine tasks and activities. For a volunteer church secretary, for example, these might include filing, typing, answering the phone, straightening and cleaning the office, etc.

7. Strengths/Gifts/Talents—In any position there are *one or two major strengths or abilities* required if the person is to do a successful job. Think this through, and be able to explain it thoroughly and clearly to candidates for the position.

(continued, page 248)

Position Focus Sheet

Person assigned:

Effective date:

1. Position title:

2. Purpose of position:

3. Reports to:

4. Relates closely with:

5. Persons responsible for:

6. Continuing responsibilities:

7. Primary strengths/gifts/talents required:

(page 1)

8. Role Preference—This refers to designations from the *Role Preference Inventory,* a testing tool from Masterplanning Group International. that helps the user define what will bring him or her maximum personal fulfillment from the job.

9. Top Three Goals—In our opinion, measurable goals for the coming year should be expected and stated for *every* position. This is one of the most valuable items of information on the position focus sheet, offering a clear picture of exactly what is expected from whoever fills the position. It makes the decision on assigning someone to the position far easier for everyone.

10. Budget—Indicate here the amount budgeted for expenditures by the person in this position. (Volunteers especially need to know what monies if any are allocated for their work expenses.)

11. Salary—If the position is a volunteer position, indicate it clearly.

12. Time Required—It is especially important to state specific expectations of time involvement to volunteers. In volunteer work the tendency is to have a person continue in a position for as long as he doesn't object to it. This is unfair, and is one of the main reasons people hesitate to volunteer. If the job is a three-month assignment, don't keep the person working in it for years, always wondering when his three months will be up! A task with a clearly indicated termination point will help give a volunteer a satisfying sense of completion when the time is over.

13. Why Position Needed—If the position is important enough to be filled, that importance should be conveyed with enthusiasm. Help the person understand from the outset the critical nature of his responsibilities.

14. Benefits—Being able to picture the personal growth and other future benefits that will come from being in this position is a key motivation to accept the assignment.

15. General Information—Put here any important aspects of the position that have not been covered above.

8. Role preference:

9. Top three measurable goals for position, for coming year:
    -
    -
    -

10. Budget available:

11. Approximate salary/honorarium: $_____ per_____

12. Approximate time required in position:

    hours per week:

    number of weeks:

    number of months:

13. Why position needed:

14. Benefits to person responsible:

15. General information:
    (Authority limits, special equipment, special requirements)

(page 2)

The Recruitment Process

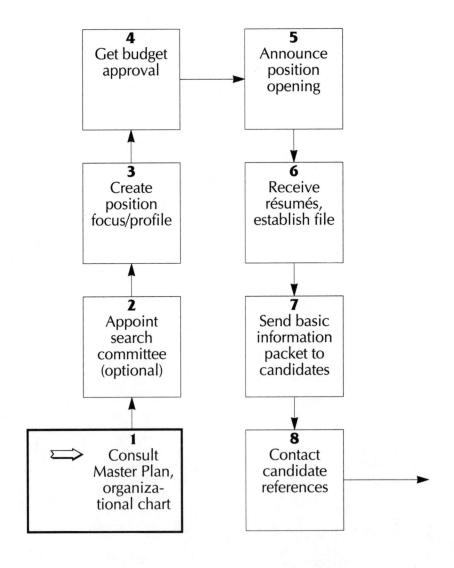

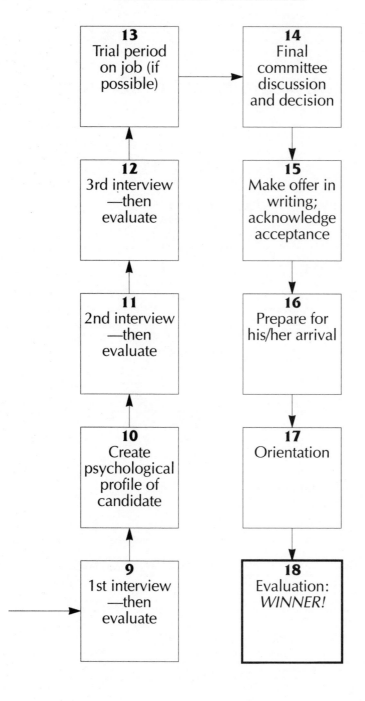

Evaluation

Annual Evaluation

A Sample Form for Staff and Board Members

Name:

Position:

Department:

Appraisal Period—from: to:

A Review of Performance Factors:

1. QUANTITY OF WORK
   Evaluate the volume of work accomplished in relation to quantity standards, regardless of quality.

Unsatisfactory	Needs Improvement		COMPETENT		Above Requirements		Distinguished
☐	☐	☐	☐	■	☐	☐	☐

2. QUALITY OF WORK
   Evaluate performance in meeting established requirements for accuracy, good judgment, and neatness.

Unsatisfactory	Needs Improvement		COMPETENT		Above Requirements		Distinguished
☐	☐	☐	☐	■	☐	☐	☐

3. KNOWLEDGE AND TECHNICAL ABILITY
   Evaluate whether the person possesses the necessary skills and knowledge for doing the job.

Unsatisfactory	Needs Improvement		COMPETENT		Above Requirements		Distinguished
☐	☐	☐	☐	■	☐	☐	☐

4. CREATIVITY AND INITIATIVE
Evaluate performance in overcoming difficult situations and initiating new ideas and constructive changes.

Unsatisfactory	Needs Improvement	COMPETENT	Above Requirements	Distinguished
☐ ☐	☐ ☐	■	☐ ☐	☐ ☐

5. LEARNING ABILITY
Evaluate ability to learn new methods and concepts, to apply new knowledge, and to retain information.

Unsatisfactory	Needs Improvement	COMPETENT	Above Requirements	Distinguished
☐ ☐	☐ ☐	■	☐ ☐	☐ ☐

6. DEPENDABILITY
Evaluate whether person can be consistently depended on to perform duties that are within the limits of his or her training and ability.

Unsatisfactory	Needs Improvement	COMPETENT	Above Requirements	Distinguished
☐ ☐	☐ ☐	■	☐ ☐	☐ ☐

7. COOPERATION
Evaluate ability to work efficiently with others; also evaluate general attitude toward the organization and toward the person's supervisor.

Unsatisfactory	Needs Improvement	COMPETENT	Above Requirements	Distinguished
☐ ☐	☐ ☐	■	☐ ☐	☐ ☐

Summary:

1. Strongest qualities:

2. Qualities most needing improvement:

3. Suggested future training and development:

4. Additional comments:

5. Summary of overall performance:

Evaluated by: Date:

Reviewed by: Date:

Signature of person evaluated:

                    Date:

After the Evaluation

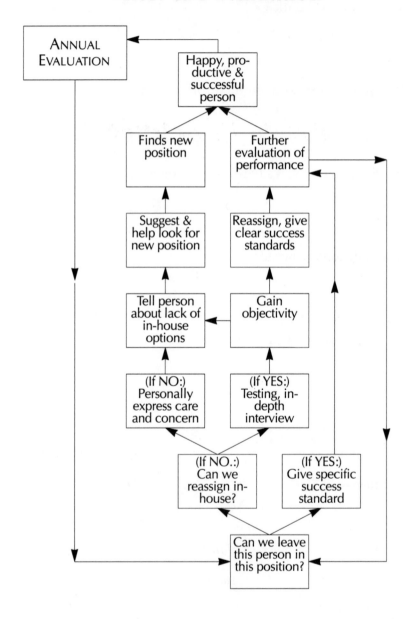

Crisis Checklist

Crisis Checklist

1. Pray…give thanks…check our motives…and give praise to God!

> *Gaining God's perspective turns panic into appreciation for God's sovereignty*

2. Put it into "big picture" context.

> *Remember the positive progress we've already made.*

3. Ask the essence question: What really is the situation?

> *Define it as concisely as possible, with the fewest number of parts and concepts*

4. Turn the sensational into simple truth.

> *Recognize and answer any falsehood, and take positive initiative. Move from a defensive to an affirmative position. Talk positively about the future.*

5. Make positive assumptions, and commit to love those involved, with genuine concern for their well-being.

> *Even in a crisis, treat everyone in a Christian manner.*

6. Identify the legal implications.

    Be wise as serpents,
    and as innocent as doves.

7. Identify the first three action steps for immediate response.

8. Communicate with simple honesty, speaking in love. Centralize the communications process, if necessary.

    Answer questions honestly...
    or not at all.

9. Hold a question-and-answer session with your top leadership team, and give an open and honest update. Answer their questions, and ask for their support.

    Asking for help says,
    "We're on the same team!"

Assumptions in a Crisis

1. People tend to communicate sensationally in a crisis.

2. What men mean for harm, God means for good.

3. If the crisis is receiving news coverage (with negative publicity), remember: The news media typically distort and misquote, and newspapers sell on sensation and fear.

4. Consider *both* these perspectives:

   > We're making too much of this.
   > We're not making enough of this.

   It's dangerous to think entirely one way or the other—until after the crisis is over.

Setting Policy

Board Policy—A Sample Statement

(The pages in this section represent pages from
a board policy manual.)

Subject: CONFLICT OF INTEREST

Summary

The purpose of this policy is to assist (name of organization) in
identifying, disclosing, and resolving potential conflicts of interest.

Scope

The following statement of policy applies to:
- each member of the Board, and
- all management and staff (hereinafter referred to as "Staff")

Fiduciary Responsibility

Members of the Board and Staff serve (name of organization) and
have a clear obligation to conduct all affairs of the Organization in
an upright and honest manner. Each person should make
necessary decisions using good judgment and Christlike ethical
and moral considerations, recognizing that "it is required that
those who have been given a trust must prove faithful" (1
Corinthians 4:2).

All decisions of the Board and Staff of the Organization are to
be made solely on the basis of a desire to promote the best
interests of Jesus Christ through this Organization and its
ministry.

Policy

Members of the Board and Staff agree to place the welfare of the
Organization above personal interests, interests of family
members, or others who may be personally involved in substantial
affairs affecting the Organization's basic functions.

Specific Disclosure

Members of the Board and Staff shall disclose fully the precise nature of their interest or involvement when participating in any transaction for the Organization in which another party to the transaction includes:

- himself or herself;
- a member of the family (spouse, parents, brothers, sisters, children, and any other immediate relatives), or,
- an organization with which the member of the Board or the Staff, or his family, is affiliated.

Disclosure shall be made at the first knowledge of the transaction.

General Disclosure

Members of the Board and Staff shall disclose all relationships and business affiliations which may now, or in the future, potentially conflict with the interests of the Organization or bring personal gain to them or their family, or business. Disclosure must be made if any member of the Board or Staff or a member of his or her family:

- is an officer, director, trustee, partner, employee, or agent of an organization with which (name of your organization) has business dealings;
- is either the actual or beneficial owner of more than one percent (1%) of the voting stock or controlling interest of an organization with which (name of your organization) has business dealings;
- is a consultant for such an organization. or,
- has any other direct or indirect dealings with an individual or organization from which he or she is materially benefitted (e.g., through the receipt directly or indirectly of cash, gifts, or other property).

Reporting of Disclosures

All disclosures required by Staff will be handled by the Vice President of Finance, and all disclosures as they apply to members of the Board shall be referred to the Secretary of the Board. Information disclosed to the Secretary of the Board or the Vice

President of Finance will be held in confidence, except when the Organization's best interests would be served by bringing the information to the attention of the Executive Committee of the Board and the officers of the Organization.

Restraint on Participation

Members of the Board and Staff who have a conflict of interest in any matter shall refrain from participating in the consideration of the proposed transaction.

The person or persons involved will not vote on such matters. However, for special reasons, the Board may request information or interpretation from the person or persons involved.

Determination of Possible Conflict of Interest

Any individual who is uncertain about a conflict of interest in any matter shall disclose such possible conflict to the appropriate individual as noted above.

Each member of the Board and the Senior Management Staff will complete and update a copy of the Organization's Disclosure Letter annually. The letter will be reviewed by the Secretary of the Board or the Vice President of Finance.

If a potential conflict of interest arises subsequent to the submission of the annual Disclosure Letter, the Board Member or Senior Management Staff is responsible for advising of such occurrence as soon as possible but not later than thirty (30) days after the occurrence. After receiving acknowledgment that the Disclosure Letter has been received, the member of the Board or Staff shall be entitled to act as though no conflict of interest exists unless he or she is notified otherwise by the Vice President of Finance or the Secretary of the Board within one hundred and twenty (120) days of filing the letter.

Failure to Disclose

Each member of the Board and the Senior Management Staff who is requested to file this Conflict of Interest Statement should recognize that such filing is a requirement for continued affiliation or employment with (name of organization) and, further, that failure to knowingly disclose a potential conflict of interest could result in disaffiliation or termination of employment.

(Signed and dated by the President and Secretary of the Board)

SAMPLE DISCLOSURE LETTER

Attn: (Secretary of the Board, Vice President of Finance, or other appropriate person)

I have received and read the Conflict of Interest policy statement approved by the Board, and to the best of my knowledge and information, I am in compliance with the policy except as specifically set forth below.

[Check the applicable circumstance:]

_____ I have no involvements, associations, financial interests, gifts, or loans to disclose.

_____ I am involved with an organization, corporation, company, or other entity with which (name of organization) has business dealings.

This category includes such things as (but is not limited to): serving as an officer or director of a company which contracts to provide goods or services to (name of organization), acting as a consultant to an organization which either receives funds from or contributes money to (name of organization), or serving in any capacity in another entity with which (name of organization) transacts business.

Name of Organization/ Corporation(s):	Office held:	Approximate dollar amount of business involved with:

For Board Research

A Survey Form for Boards

(To find out more about other boards, you can use a survey form with questions such as these:)

MEMBERSHIP

1. How many members does your board include?

voting members: _____
nonvoting members: _____

2. Is full voting membership held by the senior executive of the organization or institution your board serves?

___ no   ___ yes

3. Please describe the number of board members according to the following characteristics:

a. Sex. The number who are:

_____ male
_____ female

b. Race. The number who are:

_____ Black
_____ Caucasian
_____ Hispanic
_____ Asian
_____ other:

c. Age. The number who are:

_____ under 30 years of age
_____ in their 30s
_____ in their 40s
_____ in their 50s
_____ in their 60s
_____ age 70 or over

d. Educational background. The number whose highest educational level achieved is:

_____ less than a high school diploma
_____ high school diploma or equivalent
_____ associate's degree (A.S., A.A.)
_____ bachelor's degree (B.A., B.S.)
_____ master's degree (M.A., M.Div., M.S.)
_____ doctorate (Ed.D, Ph.D.)
_____ professional degree (D.Min, J.D., M.D.)
_____ honorary doctorate

e. Occupational background. The number of board members whose *primary* occupation is (count each board member once):

_____ finance and insurance
_____ general business and industry
_____ nonprofit organization
_____ education (teaching or administration)
_____ medical and other health services
_____ law/government
_____ skilled trade or service
(continued)

_____ homemaking
_____ social services
_____ clergy
_____ communications/
journalism
_____ agriculture
_____ fine arts
_____ retired
_____ other:

f. Income level. The number
of board members whose
estimated annual personal
income is:

_____ less than $25,000
_____ $25,000 to $49,999
_____ $50,000 to $74,999
_____ $75,000 to $99,999
_____ $100,000 or more

g. Residence. The number of
board members who are
estimated to reside the
following distance from the
organization or institution:

_____ local
_____ not local but within 100
miles
_____ from 100 to 500 miles
_____ more than 500 miles

4. Please indicate the number
of board members who
currently serve in the
following capacities (check
all that apply):

_____ board member of a
corporation
_____ member of the governing
board of another
organization or institution.
_____ chairman or president of a
corporation
_____ major administrator of
another organization or
institution

5. Please indicate the number
of years that constitute a
term of office for a board
member?

___ one year
___ two years
___ three years
___ four years
___ five years
___ other:

6. Are board members limited
in the consecutive number
of terms they may serve?

___ no ___ yes

If "yes," what number? _____

BOARD MEETINGS

7. How is the chairperson of
the board selected?

___ chosen by the board
___ appointed by:

___ other:

8. Is there a requirement
concerning the number of
full board meetings which
must be held annually?

___ no requirement
___ once per year
___ twice per year
___ quarterly
___ monthly
___ other:

(continued)

9. How often, typically, are full board meetings held each year?

___ once per year
___ twice per year
___ quarterly
___ monthly
___ other:

10. How long is the average business meeting of the full board?

___ two hours
___ half day (a three- to four-hour session)
___ one day
___ two to three days
___ other:

11. How many board members attend an average meeting of the full board?

number attending, on average:

_____

average number as a percentage of full board membership:
_____%

12. How many executive staff or officers from the organization or institution served by the board typically attend a full board meeting?

number attending, on average:

_____

Please indicate the positions held by these executive staff or officers:

___ Senior Executive
___ others:

EXECUTIVE COMMITTEE

13. Is there an executive committee (or equivalent) of the board?

___ no   ___ yes

If "yes," how often does it meet?

___ twice a month
___ monthly
___ quarterly
___ semi-annually
___ only on matters of urgency
___ other:

STANDING COMMITTEES

14. Does the board maintain standing committees (or subcommittees)?
___ no
___ yes

If "yes," please list each subcommittee's area of concern:

A Salary Survey Form

Position or Level:	Senior Executive	Level 2	Level 3	Level 4	Level 5	Level 6
Number in position:						
Monthly salary range:						
(check:) Salary increased by...						
• merit raise only						
• automatic raise only						
• part merit, part automatic						
Education						
Job Categories & Descriptions						

OTHER SALARY INCOME:

	(YES)	(NO)

1. Do you have a cost-of-living allowance included in salary rates? _____ | _____

2. Do you give bonus or incentive payment? (If yes, average amount included: $_____ per _____) _____ | _____

3. Do you provide an automobile allowance? (If yes, what amount per mile? _____) _____ | _____

4. Do you provide a housing allowance? _____ | _____

   (If yes, does amount vary with each house?) _____ | _____

5. Do you make other provisions for job expenses? (If yes, please explain:) _____ | _____

6. Do you have a child allowance? _____ | _____

7. Do you allow employees to keep honorariums? _____ | _____

8. Do you give sabbatical leaves? (If yes, please explain:) _____ | _____

9. Do you have available a loan fund or credit union from which employees can borrow? _____ | _____

10. What is your schedule for paid vacations?
    _____ weeks after _____
    _____ weeks after _____
    _____ weeks after _____

11. How many paid holidays are granted per year? _____

12. How much sick leave with full pay is given? _____ days per year

13. Insurance: ___ hospital and surgical
    ___ life: (amount: _____; employee pays _____%)
    ___ long-term disability
    ___ pension plan (How long must employee work to be eligible? _____) Percent employee pays monthly: _____

14. Social Security: Percent employee pays monthly: _____

15. Indicate other benefits (such as dental and eye care):

277

More Resources

Books by Ted W. Engstrom

A TIME FOR COMMITMENT, Zondervan, 1987

FOR THE WORKAHOLIC I LOVE (with David J. Juroe), Revell, 1979 (previously published as THE WORK TRAP)

INTEGRITY (with Robert C. Larson), Word, 1987

MANAGING YOUR TIME (with R. Alec MacKenzie), Zondervan, 1967

MOTIVATION TO LAST A LIFETIME (with Robert C. Larson), Zondervan, 1984

60-SECOND MANAGEMENT GUIDE (with Edward R. Dayton), Word, 1984

STRATEGY FOR LEADERSHIP (with Edward R. Dayton), Revell, 1979

STRATEGY FOR LIVING (with Edward R. Dayton), Regal, 1979

THE ART OF MANAGEMENT FOR CHRISTIAN LEADERS (with Edward R. Dayton), Word, 1976

TED ENGSTROM: MAN WITH A VISION (with Bob Owen),
Tyndale, 1984

THE CHRISTIAN EXECUTIVE (with Edward R. Dayton),
Word, 1979

THE FINE ART OF FRIENDSHIP (with Robert C. Larson),
Thomas Nelson, 1985

THE MAKING OF A CHRISTIAN LEADER, Zondervan,
1976

THE PURSUIT OF EXCELLENCE, Zondervan, 1982

THE WORK TRAP, Revell, 1979

WHAT IN THE WORLD IS GOD DOING? (with David J.
Juroe), Word, 1978

YOUR GIFT OF ADMINISTRATION, Thomas Nelson, 1983

Leadership Resources from Masterplanning Group International

"A" CHART

Your year of planning and programming at a glance—all of your major events with planning lead time shown. Space for up to 40 major events down the left side of the chart, and the next 12 months across the top. Helps you keep track of several events all happening the same month, but requiring many planning deadlines over several months; all in one clear annual ("A") overview. Key tool if you keep a busy, complex schedule.

ART OF ASKING

Helps you ask penetrating, powerful, practical questions at the right time. Teaches you the process of creating good questions and explains why effective questioning is so fundamental to top leadership. Contains more than three hundred ready-to-use questions.

BOARDS—HOW TO WORK EFFECTIVELY WITH YOUR BOARD

This compact paper spells out a practical step-by-step approach to preparing for, running, and following up an effective board meeting.

BOARDS—HOW TO ASK THE "HARD QUESTIONS"

Questions to ask before making a major decision in direction, staffing, or finances.

CAREER CHANGE—30 QUESTIONS

Thirty questions to help you any time you're thinking about making a career or position change.

CASH FLOW PROJECTIONS

A simple, practical tool for forecasting income, expenses, and net on a monthly basis.

DELEGATION SHEETS

A simple sheet for keeping information about the staff member's projects, goals, milestones, and continuing activities.

DIVORCE—30 QUESTIONS

A list of questions to ask *before* deciding on a divorce. A strong counseling aid to objective thinking.

EMOTIONAL BALANCE CHART

An 11" x 17" chart that allows you to study your emotional patterns, maximizing your sense of emotional stability.

ENCOURAGING YOURSELF AND OTHERS

"Who encourages the encourager?" Frequently leaders have no one to encourage them when they need just that. *Encouraging Y and O* describes a process for gaining perspective on life, which brings encouragement—so you in turn can encourage others.

EVENT PLANNING CHECKLIST

A 300-point checklist to help you ask all the right questions when planning any event or retreat.

EXECUTIVE EVALUATION—135

A comprehensive, positive evaluation checklist for use with staff or close friends.

EXECUTIVE "PROBE" QUESTIONS

Penetrating questions you can ask to stay focused on your highest priorities.

FILING AND INDEXING FOR SMALL OFFICES

A simple, but clarifying paper on the subject of filing.

FOCUSING YOUR LIFE IN ONE DAY

Notebook and cassette tapes offering help in gaining clear direction in seven areas of your life.

GLOSSARY OF MASTERPLANNING TERMS

Glossary of 122 terms your team can use to develop a common language, preventing misunderstandings and team conflict.

GOD'S CALLING—COUNTING THE COST

Ideas and questions to consider before leaving an established position in business and plunging into fulltime Christian work.

IDENTITY CHART

Lets you look at your past, present and possible future positions and see how the primary dimensions of your identity will be affected by the changes you are considering.

LEADERSHIP INVENTORY

Helps you see where each of your staff members (paid or volunteer) feels he wants to grow in his leadership skills.

LEADING WITH WISDOM

A 105-page workbook with eight hours of audio cassette training tapes covering thirty areas of leadership, including: How to cope with change, failure, loneliness, pressure; How to become more balanced, creative, and disciplined; How to develop effective skills in communicating, decision making, goal setting, delegating, and team building.

LIFE BALANCE CHART

This 24" x 36" chart gives you an overview of seven dimensions of your life—spiritual, physical, personal growth, family/marriage, social, professional/career, and financial.

LIFE FOCUS SHEETS

What do you want to *be, do, have,* and who do you want to *help* before you die? This single sheet helps you develop a clear life focus in a relatively short time (frequently less than one hour). Once your long-term focus is clear, developing a specific plan to get there is far easier.

LIFE INVENTORY

In only a few minutes, this inventory can help you spot fundamental problems a friend or team member may be having.

LIFELONG FRIENDS LIST

A systematic way of keeping track of your friends year after year.

LIFENOTES

A notebook designed to capture your thinking. With thirty different categories, you'll have "a place for every thought, and (ultimately) every thought in it's place!" An excellent way to keep track of your best thoughts, hopes, and dreams.

LISTENING

Why do some people hear the things other people miss? This series is for the person who wants seriously to become a skilled listener.

MEMORIES—A PRICELESS HEIRLOOM

A family heirloom that contains more than five hundred questions to help your parents or grandparents remember and record all the memorable events of their life. It's a beautiful book with leather-like binding and gilt-edged pages.

POSITION FOCUS SHEET

Lets you spell out clearly the basic relationships and responsibilities of an organizational position.

PRESIDENTIAL SERIES: PRESIDENTIAL SELLING

There's a big transition from being a salesman trying to present himself as a president, to being a president who knows how to sell. There's also a major advantage in looking at the subject of sales from a presidential perspective. This notebook and two hours of audio cassette tapes covers thirty years of successful selling experience.

PROCESS CHARTING

Process charting may be the most valuable and least understood skill in leadership today. A clear understanding of process charting provides a framework for fundamental organizational development.

PROFILE SYSTEM

A single sheet for keeping track of all the "little insights" and major discoveries about close friends, family members, or staff.

PROJECT FOCUS SHEET

Keeps the many pieces of any new project in focus.

PROPOSAL WRITING QUESTIONS

Forty-two questions you can expect any foundation or major donor to ask.

QUICK FOCUS SHEETS

If you feel out of focus at times (as most leaders do), this can help you refocus your life in fifteen minutes.

RECRUITING EXECUTIVE STAFF

A notebook/cassette tape series covering the 18-step recruiting process. Questions to help maximize your ability to choose the right person for the right position.

REPORTING

Explains the reasons for regular staff reporting and covers all of the key questions to ask in the process.

ROLE PREFERENCE INVENTORY

A key to selecting the right person for the position; it also helps you identify what you *want* to do, as opposed to what you *can* do or *have* to do.

SCRIPTURAL MEDITATION

A book to help you grow deeper in your personal walk with the Lord Jesus Christ.

A SINGLE YEAR

A list of prioritizing questions to ask yourself on your birthday, New Year's Day, or whenever you feel foggy about your own personal priorities.

STRATEGY WORK SHEETS

This 11" x 17" worksheet is extremely helpful in thinking through the step-by-step process you or your staff members go through in moving from setting a goal to reaching it, and declaring it a successful milestone. Helps you spot problems in your staff's strategies before they become costly.

TRAILMARKS

Twenty-five proven principles for helping staff sort out problems, make decisions, and understand why things work as they do.

WISDOM LIST

A list of two hundred often used bits of wisdom (principles, rules of thumb, observations).

YOU-FOCUS

If you could double the effectiveness of all your communications for your lifetime by investing two hours and $50, would it be worth it? Every area of your life requiring communication will benefit from this series: your speaking, teaching, letter writing, materials creation, television/radio work, and counseling.

For a complete free Resource Catalogue, write to:

Masterplanning Group International
Post Office Box 6128
Laguna Niguel, California 92677

Telephone: (714) 495-8850